Homeless to Happy in a Split Second

by Julie Cara Hoffenberg

Foreword by Peter Ragnar

Edited by Meg Easling

Disclaimer: This book is intended for informational purposes only. It is not meant to diagnose, cure, treat or heal any health concerns. Please consult a professional for any and all health concerns. Julie Cara Hoffenberg, her business, and associates are released of any responsibility in your personal choices as a result of reading this book. The author has also made every effort to ensure internet sources and information are correct at the time of publishing. The author does not have any control over and does not assume any responsibility for author or third-party websites or their content.

Homeless to Happy in a Split Second
Some names and/or locations have been changed to honor privacy. No part of this book may be reproduced, stored in a retrieval system, or transmitted in any form, by any means, including mechanical, electronic, photocopying, recording or otherwise, without prior written permission from and credit to the author.

by Julie Cara Hoffenberg
Foreword by Peter Ragnar
Edited by Meg Easling
Publisher - Julie Cara Hoffenberg
P.O. Box 293 Ojai, California 93024
www.JulieCaraHoffenberg.com
www.JuliesSpiritualJourney.com
Library of Congress Control Number: 2019911889
ISBN Number: 978-1-7333082-0-5

CONTENTS

APPRECIATIONS

I am thankful, grateful, and appreciative to the following wise owls, kind kittens, and courageous bears in my life. Together you gather as a great beacon of light, guiding me further home to my heart and what I really want to share with this world.

Mom - Thank you for bringing life to my cells, family to my soul, and the masses of love and help over the years. I've been blessed greatly to have you in my life and I love you unconditionally. May our "cawfee tawks" continue for a lifetime!

Dad - To the person in my memory, the one who was there for me in every way.

Kevin Trudeau and my GIN Family - Thank you for the support, cognitions, and friendships that will last a lifetime. You have inspired me to stick with many things I was ready to give up on, one of them being myself. I love you all deeply.

Peter Ragnar and my Good Luck Family - Peter, thank you for the purity of your spirit. It's your pathless path, wordless words, and congruent life that inspire me on continuous levels. Family, thank you for your support, encouragement, and consciousness. How blessed we all are to share our circle.

My real life Angels:

Jo and Ross - You are family to me always. Thank you for the financial help, for storing my crap, and the delicious breakfasts over tears and smiles. I love you.

Randee - You're my Ojai MaMa. Thank you for getting my mail and all the talks. You know my heart and I love you dearly.

Gary - The $100 you slipped me as I left town was more of a revolution that you will likely never understand, and so is your friendship and abundance consciousness. You're rad.

Amber and Kurt - Thank you for a landing place, regardless of where I am in life and the support with my rent when I was short. I love you guys. You're in my heart perpetually.

Carl - You were also a rent angel who helped me when I needed it. Thank you for your trust in my ability to keep my word and pay you back.

Mitra and Marjan - You tried to be anonymous rent angels, but I knew it was you. How could it not be with those caring, beautiful hearts so full of love? I treasure you, my friends.

Cousins Paul, Sherry, and Stuart - I'm grateful for your trust when I asked for help. You were part of my healing journey and I'm so blessed to have family like you.

Lokpal - Thank you for my crystals, towel, soap, the healing sessions, and most of all the blessing of being of service to the group. I'm forever grateful and am hugging you in my heart.

My Beloved, Carol - I thought this book would be published long before we ever met. There's no accident it's all happening now. You support my writing in a way I had wished for in a partner. I'm so grateful to be on this adventure with you, a time of "revolutionary love" and awakening. Thank you for all of the ways you've gifted me like no one else has. You're a remarkable Lemurian, my love.

There are many other angels who walked along the path with me over the last year or more. I'm so grateful to all of you for your love and guidance.

With love,

Julie xo

FOREWORD

Julie's brutal self-honesty can be both scary and refreshing to the readers of this amazing adventure. Many people are fearful because of being so centered in outward appearances that life may appear hollow, but in this book you get to see life from the inside out. As Julie points out, the more we distance ourselves from our core values, the emptier we feel. Her adventure takes us on the trail in "Poops, Paws and Sweet Liberation," not just to huge paw prints in the sand, but onward to surrender and walking the spiritual path. You're also getting a great reading list as you go along.

I think it's easy for many of us to get a negative or knee-jerk reaction to anyone's homeless experience, but what I enjoyed was the different perspective that Julie put on it. She addresses loss and happiness, transition and hope, and tags each chapter with a quote.

She addresses judgment from a very candid place in "I'm Still Judgmental (Sometimes)." We also get to meet Julie's friends through these pages. In a way it's a bit like Kerouac's *On the Road*. Through these pages we travel from Ojai and the California coast to the redwoods and beyond, from hugging saints to learning to trust oneself.

You may be surprised with "Ten Reasons To Live In Your Car," and come to realize it's not what you might think. This is all about the choices we choose to make in order to find our personal freedom and taste. Her love of nature and animals is ever present through these pages. Imagine spending a year traveling some of the most scenic coastline in America with Julie. Well, that's what you're about to do as you turn these pages.

Peter Ragnar, Author of Finding Heart – How to Live With Courage in a Confusing World

INTRODUCTION – FROM THE INSIDE OUT

December, 2013 - Bleeding from the Inside Out

My right hand knuckles are bleeding.

I glance down at them.

Ouch.

I can feel they will be bruised and swollen, as I cannot open and close my fist with fluidity.

Tears are exploding

> *from*

> > *my*

> > > *eyes.*

*I watch the garden hose spray water into the obsidian night sky, aimlessly, with no purpose. I am **not** doing a good job of watering the yard. This is merely a way to connect with the earth in a state of desperation. I cry out to the infinite multi-verse stretched above me, "Aaaahhhhhhh!"*

Ouch.

I can see more bits of blood forming where each big knuckle bends. The porch light illuminates them and I cringe at the thought of becoming someone who punches a wall out of anger.

"Who am I?" I think.

"Who was the person that did something so immature and silly? How can an intelligent, conscious, loving being such as myself do something like this?"

I consider for a moment that the person punching the wall is not "me". I consciously vow never to allow this to happen again and to release and heal all that caused this.

I sob loudly, talking to myself. No one can hear me except, potentially, my partner who is resting on the other side of the window (and the neighbors). I know she can't hear my words, but she can definitely hear my pain.

Ouch. My knuckles swell.

I continue to cry and spray things I'm not supposed to, such as the chairs and the clean windows. I'm angrier than I've ever been before. I'm angry for the person I allowed myself to become physically, mentally, and emotionally. I know better than this. I teach people how to do and be better than this. I'm angry at having failed most of what I created in my life. I failed with my two businesses, I failed to hold the steady job and get good benefits that my family taught me are of the utmost importance. I failed to leave several emotionally toxic relationships sooner, knowing I could have prevented what I felt presently. I failed to stay connected to the truth of who I am. I failed to visit family due to lack of funds to visit them. I failed to have the money to go out with friends and felt ashamed that I had to keep saying "no" to their events. I failed to pay all my credit cards immediately so that I could carry a zero balance. I failed to make rent and had to cash in my retirement over the last few years for this and other reasons.

I didn't want to die. I didn't want to actually hurt myself. It's just that my emotions swelled into such a pronounced wave that they exploded in the result of me punching that damn wall!

Ouch. My knuckles are really hurting. I better put some ice on them.

March, 2014 - Working from the Outside In

A great purging sensation came over me as a result of admitting my failures and anger toward myself and others. I took a lot of action, swearing I was going to go out and "get a bunch of money" with my new Life Insurance position. After all, I met one of the most successful Life Insurance agents ever, so obviously money would come rolling into my life if I followed his lead. Although I did not realize it at the time, my inner voice was calling for a lifestyle of freedom (but more on that later). All I wanted was to have enough money in the bank to do what I wanted, such as writing, traveling, art, speaking, and sharing with people. Life Insurance was to be my nest egg. I would use the saved funds from insurance to launch what I really wanted to do.

Everything I did was fueled from this anger of being broke, coupled with the anger and sadness of breaking up with my partner. We were both loving, wonderful souls but could not be together any longer. I was asking myself questions like, "How is it humanly possible that love can be brought into our lives that is both the most tender and beautiful thing imaginable, and also the most toxic and dangerous? How much pain could I have saved us if I never got into the relationship in the first place? Perhaps it's good that I experienced the relationship, or else I would not have felt the depth of connection I did?"

I was desperate and searched (externally) for answers to both my financial problems and to living a life that was aligned with my gifts. At the time, I did not realize I was creating more of the same situations and looking for answers in other programs or people.

For example, the gentleman who introduced me to Life Insurance was not someone I would necessarily "follow" if I was truly listening to my gut. He was a good man, with good values, and had a good family. He was, truly, a wonderful person. He made big money. He had nice clothes. He looked good and smelled good. But several times I realized that he never questioned me about who I am, what I like, or what makes me tick. He virtually ignored me on a drive one night and had I listened to that stillness within, it would have kept me from delving into a business and a mentor I did not ultimately resonate with. My gut spoke to me the very first time this man spoke at a success meeting we attended. He spoke for a very long time about himself, which was not what was recommended by the group. We were to be brief and respectful of the other people there. But I didn't listen to the lack of resonance I felt. I knew immediately he was just a bit too into himself. I knew immediately, the way he flashed wads of money in his brief case, spoke of insecurity. The truly abundant have nothing to prove. A great teacher of mine once said, "Do not be deceived by your ears and eyes. A person can look good, smell good, and talk good, but if you don't get the right *feeling*, move on."

But I didn't listen! I got my insurance license in the summer of 2013. Almost a year later, I was still struggling in the business. I was looking at numbers. Every day I would think, "If I can just set such-and-such number of appointments, I will make such-and-such amount of money and my problems will be over. Then I would feel sick, knowing I hated the selling tactics I was being taught. So when it came time to making calls, I'd haul off to the beach for a walk or curl up in my car with one too many chocolate bars and slices of cheese. Once in a while, I would set an appointment and end up talking about spirituality, personal development, or health with my clients. (Almost all of them were on one to twenty, yes *twenty*, toxic pharmaceutical drugs. They had trouble getting life insurance because the insurance companies saw a huge risk in most heavily medicated people.) I laughed hysterically with one client whose daughter was a lesbian and somehow a rainbow sticker on the refrigerator brought us into a discussion of my own "gayness" as they put it. From there we thought up smoothie recipes and very little insurance work was done. I was, indeed, using my gifts (which had absolutely nothing to do with selling insurance).

One of my mentors at the time taught me a few things about beliefs. We were discussing that no matter how much you think you will do something, if it does not align with what you believe, you will not do it. I had some major cognitions about this, as my beliefs were: We should be honest with clients, be respectful of their wishes when they give us an answer, and be transparent instead of trying to pull something over their eyes. Because I was being taught the opposite of the beliefs that were imprinted deep in my soul, I would wake up and dread doing the activity that could yield my pay. This just made me feel worse about myself, feeling as though I failed yet again. I don't want to insinuate that the creator of the huge brokerage we all worked under was all bad. We were not only taught terrible selling tactics. Much of what I learned was fantastic. But nonetheless, there were several things we were encouraged to do that had nothing to do with the integrity of sales I resonated with.

Just before summer, I realized Life Insurance was not something that aligned with my soul. What was I going to do?

This is the key point - *I searched again. Externally.* From the outside in. I searched for "work". I picked up a summer camp job, which paid a couple months of rent. I attracted house sitting and pet sitting jobs, which I loved, but they do *not* pay the rent.

The months flew by and my lease was ending in August, at which point my ex and I would be moving out. One of the months I could not pay any rent at all and sent a message out to most of the people I knew, asking them to donate one hundred dollars to help me and promised to pay it back. It was both a horrifying experience and also a very therapeutic one. It provided me the opportunity to feel the shame when I initially sent the email, and the release of it as I saw all the loving reflections sent back my way. A realization occurred that my soul is not the sum total of the dollars I've gained and lost. I saw that the true friends, family, and angels in our lives "judge not" and give from the heart without lecture. They even went a step further by appreciating the vulnerability and conveying how my email helped them go within. It was painful and powerful on more levels than I have space to list here.

As August approached, I still did not have "work". Where was my "work"? I needed "work"! It must be somewhere! Maybe under that cushion, over the hill, or left at the gas station. This is what society often teaches us about "finding work". You look for something outside of you. I was certainly following suit and looking from the outside in.

August, 2014 - Living from the Inside Out

I sat on a wrestling mat on the hardwood floor of my three bedroom, two bath home. In one hour, the mat would be packed into my car and would become my bed. Everything I owned was placed in a 5' x 10' storage unit. My cat had been dropped off with a foster parent since my ex would be living somewhere she could not keep animals. Handing off my cat was an experience I would liken to sledge hammering my heart. But I also knew something was changing in a positive way. I took a deep breath in, feeling a sense of surrender and adventure.

The realization that there was no money to get a "new" place after I left the house was at first sobering, but it instantly turned into a feeling of freedom. There was a place deep within that craved total freedom, no rent, no one to answer to, no utilities, an opportunity to catch up on credit card bills - life on the open road! Because I felt such deep emotions about this freedom, it came rushing in. Be careful what you ask for! Most people do not want to be homeless when they are craving a life of freedom, but for me it was different. I didn't *feel* homeless. I felt like a part of me came home to myself, my desires, and a higher purpose. I stepped into my car, backed out of the driveway - and in essence, *I went from homeless to happy in a split second*!

I had a few bucks in my account from my summer camp job. There was enough to carry me through the next couple of months *if* I did odd jobs here and there. Luckily, more pet sitting came through. I even cleaned the home of my friend which was crawling with ants and soaked with urine in the restrooms. It was a bit horrifying, but I kept repeating my daily request, "Please help me be of service today and spread light through the use of my gifts."

Sometimes the lightwork was done through mundane things like cleaning that house. Other days it was done by picking up a book for my dear friend, Jo, that I knew she would love. (As a side note, I would like to share that I am quite possibly one of the best book manifestors in the world! I always find great books for fifty cents. I love books, so they love me!)

Because I had a lot of spare time, I began to take care of my soul. Trying to "find a job" was not working and I felt awful. I had forgotten, after numerous years of studying personal development, the law of attraction, and spirituality, that we create what we desire through our emotions. And when we connect with emotions that relate to our sense of passion and purpose, we begin to see the external realizations of those feelings and transmissions.

My previous attempts at trying to "find work" from the outside in were fruitless. Living in my car allowed me the opportunity to begin *living from the inside out*. Each morning I did what my soul craved. If it craved solitude, I hauled off to a trail to watch the faeries. If it craved connection, I laughed hysterically with friends or curled up on their couches after some great philosophizing (you know who you are, my dear angel-friends). I journaled often. I asked myself what I truly could give to the world.

Three words constantly come up when I ask my higher self what I can help people with - *nature*, *connection*, and *purpose*. I know, in the depth of my soul, that through my writing, communication skills, and intuitive skills, I can encourage people to live the lives they dream of.

When I observe other people who live the lives they dream of, they always have some connection to nature, connection to their inner truth and other people, and a sense of purpose (or a gift they came to share). "Purpose" tends to be a big buzz word these days and I don't wish to convey that we all must find a purpose external to ourselves. For me, purpose is more about a sense of alignment, or being "on path". It's more like an "on or off" switch (I'm either aligned or not aligned.), rather than one specific thing we came here to do. Some of my "on purpose" days are spent meditating at the ocean, even though I'm not "giving" anything to anyone. Other days I'm "on purpose" by speaking my truth to a group of people. I know people who have the ultimate purpose of sharing their zest for living with others. Purposeful living is really nothing more than feeling aligned with what your gut or soul desires to express through living. This sense of alignment, or purpose, began to awaken in me as the days carried on.

There was a period of time during which I quit "looking" for work. I simply *let go* and did all that made my heart sing. I returned to the things I loved, like reading books and listening to enlightening material. Most nights were spent on couches or pet sitting, but a few nights were spent sleeping in my small SUV. I showered at friends' houses and sometimes at the state beaches. Luckily, southern California is mild in temperature, so there were no icicle-laden eye lashes in the morning to deal with.

My money carried me through November, at which point I had the inner guidance to apply for work outside of the town I was residing in. I craved the redwoods and the water (Ojai had been in a long-term drought). As I sent out applications and resumes, I put very little energy into it. I simply sent them out like a robot, attempting to send them to companies I resonated with on some level. I thought about my purpose, my desires, and told the universe to place me where I can be of service and be aligned, ethically, with the practices and values of the company. There was one city whose name resonated with me instantly - Redwood City (Didn't I just say I was craving the redwoods!?). I got tingles when I thought about it. Keep in mind that I had never been there or heard of the city before a job opening surfaced there.

A week or so later, a woman from a health food market called me from this city that sounded wonderful. A week after that I drove the six hours to interview. A week later, I got the job and started within days. It all *felt* very free and soulful. I would be able to help people align with their health and live a better life emotionally, mentally, and physically. And while I am not the owner of my own business exclusively, without the need for a job right now, I am building a business in the meantime and feel aligned with the ethics of the current people I work for and with. I also live in the redwoods and can dash off to nature for an adventure anytime I want.

I created all of this by aligning with the true source and supply of abundance - the inner divine wisdom. This concept is so eloquently put by John Randolph Price in *The Abundance Book*. He writes, "I keep my mind and thoughts off 'this world' and I place my entire focus on God within as the only Cause of my prosperity. I acknowledge the Inner Presence as the only activity in my financial affairs, as the substance of all things visible. I place my faith in the Principle of Abundance in action within me."

I understand that aligning with the Inner Presence doesn't mean I can just kick back and suck my thumbs, expecting a job to arrive. It simply means that when I wish to create something I desire, it is to be created from the inside out, not the reverse. The last few months I spent cruising around in my truck allowed me the time to drop into the deepest, most divine aspect of myself, thereby creating from a place of inner truth, harmony, and joy.

Today is December 14th, 2014. It's been *exactly* four months since I left my house, but what I've found is my home. It lives in a place that can't be destroyed or expected to pay rent. What I've come to "know" is that I am on a spiritual journey and no longer a physical one. I also am beginning to understand that my spiritual journey truly started when I reached a place of surrender. How many people, when faced with the reality of moving into their truck, will smile and feel a surge of excitement run through them? How many people will surrender to the opportunity versus grieve the losses?

I still stay in my truck, as I cannot afford a living space yet (I work in one of the most expensive cities in the country.). But I do not focus on this. I focus on the following facts: For the first time in a few years, I paid myself ten percent of my paycheck into my savings account. As of my second work paycheck, I have entirely eliminated the need for credit card purchases. I am grateful for my gym pass, which allows me showers and saunas as needed. I am avidly saving up to see my dear family across the country and spiritual nature journeys around the world. I've seen more in the last four months than most people see in several years. I am blessed with the dearest friends, family, and mentors imaginable and I send thanks to all of them.

———

The insights I've had over the last few years have been explosive, gentle, profound, subtle, wild, and everything in between. Many of them will be shared in the blog entries that make up this book (they were originally posted on my website).

Something really powerful stands out to me right now, however. Someone I know told me I know nothing of depression. We had many conversations about emotions, medication, and natural healing modalities in the past. She told me I've never known pain so great I can't get out of bed, or a pain so great I can't imagine going on living. And if I did ever experience those pains, I'd understand that the "natural stuff" doesn't *ever* work and that most depressed people are "disabled" and must be medicated. While this may be true for some people, I knew it wasn't true for everyone.

Somewhere in me I knew differently, even when I was emotionally balanced. I've watched miracle healings by people of any and all mental/emotional backgrounds. And I now had my own proof of what was achievable given the commitment and desire to achieve it. If I had not punched a wall, cried myself into numbness, watched weeks and week of television, unable to move, dipping into and out of the big void called "despair", I would not have brought back the "medicine" I can now share with others. The silver lining is truly held amidst the darkest places we go. While I did not want to, specifically, kill myself, I did want to disappear. Life was less than a desirable experience for quite some time. I wanted to "not exist" anymore during the deepest pain I experienced. I did not get out of bed. I experienced the feelings this person described.

I healed myself entirely using all of my training in metaphysics, personal development, the law of attraction, nature, and countless years spent reading and sharing with other conscious people. I had coached people from depression to joy, from fat to thin, from anorexic to freedom with food, from purposeless to directional. But I hadn't truly brought myself from a void to filled with joy, excitement, purpose, and a newfound self-love using nothing but my thoughts, nature, physical activity, and support of loved ones.

I remember lying on the couch, not wanting to kill myself through harm, but I indeed prayed saying, "I cannot do this anymore. Please remove me from this planet. It is too dense, too much, and I cannot go on like this anymore."

From that moment, a rebirth took place. That rebirth was the exact recipe I gained as the remedy to the despair I experienced. The yin and the yang. The good and the bad. The pain and the triumph over it. Below is the exact recipe of how I pulled myself out of a void *without the need for medication or anything people told me is the "answer" to depression*. I share this with you, not only in hopes it may touch someone's life and give them a recipe for a new life, but also because it led me to the place where being faced with homelessness became irrelevant.

1. I allowed myself rest, depression, and copious hours of television. What we resist persists. I was trained to resist the possibility that I could be anything less than happy perpetually. Allowing for the human emotions threw light on my darkest place. So I let myself watch anything I wanted that made me feel good (or at least engaged). I watched cooking shows, nature programs, singing shows, dancing, etc. I had no energy and allowed myself this. I even remember texting my Mom not to contact me for a while because I felt I had culminated into everything she ever taught me was a failure - debt, no job, no benefits, no money. I told her I was in a bad place and didn't want to talk to anyone. She said I wasn't a failure and she understood. She respected the space I needed to allow my

misery to rear its head, which I appreciated. The nugget to be gained here is to allow for the feelings you feel, retreat when needed, stay honest with yourself and others, and recognize the depression for what it is. (For me, this is the beginning of triumph over the ego. The ego does not want to admit or face the reality of what is taking place. Allowing oneself to be vulnerable and seen, and to accept what is truly taking place allows the true self to begin revealing itself.)

2. After several weeks (or possibly months) of resting and staring into space, I got mad. (I used Esther Hicks' tool she and Abraham describe in *Ask and it is Given* by working my way up the emotional scale. Anger was one step up from depression/despair). I got mad at myself. I got mad at my failures. I got mad at my ex. I got mad at everything! I screamed the loudest screams imaginable, from the deepest primal power point in my soul. I'd retreat to my car and scream so loud my vocal chords became sore. I felt a rage of a thousand lifetimes leave me and I was incredibly spent afterwards. My hands took a serious beating from pounding the steering wheel as I screamed out to the ocean. I told the world I was "effing" mad and wouldn't be having anymore bullshit in my life.

3. I started walking again. I had been stagnant. A stagnant body is equal to stagnant emotions. I began to go for walks along the water and breathe. My joints hurt from not moving for so long and gaining so much weight. I walked myself out of the pain. I was still mad, but a little bit of peace crept in, the more I walked. (I recommend looking into past research studies on walking versus medication for depression, should you have interest.)

4. I went back to nature and did things I loved. At this point, my ex and I lost our home we were renting and went our separate ways. Moving into my car, as I mentioned earlier, was the catalyst to having time in nature. I knew I could enjoy nature almost constantly. Who wants to sit in a parked car all day? I went to the trees, the water, and the fresh air. I stayed with a friend on a ranch and hugged goats. I allowed myself to melt into what I loved. Nature is my bliss, thus I had reconnected with my bliss fountain!

I must state this disclaimer as well: I am not a doctor. I am not giving medical advice. I am sharing about my own personal journey out of a desolate place. I launched myself out of that place through natural protocols I was told almost "never" work. In a world where we trust our doctors more than ourselves, more than our innate healing abilities, and more than our intuition, I find it critically necessary to share every path of triumph through natural healing. The more alternates we share to drugs, years of therapy, and placing total faith in our doctors over our own guts, the better off we will be. Let us share all we can. Jump for joy when someone finds a way through the sludge to brighter days with tools that do no harm. I am not stating any of this in judgment of what your personal guidance system tells you to do, but I am most certainly backing all options that empower and do no harm. We are told drugs and countless years of therapy are "normal" and the alternates are very "dangerous" options. Make careful choices. Get quiet and check in with yourself. Perhaps it's been years since you asked yourself what you think and feel. We ask doctors, family, magazines, books, and the internet, but do we ask ourselves and listen quietly for the responses?

I'm so grateful for the medicine I found. I'm so grateful for the depth of pain I experienced that led to a real experience of healing myself naturally with the tools I had only studied about in years previous.

The greatest bit of medicine I brought back from the darkness was the knowingness that we must *desire* and *believe* that healing is possible before attempting it. The well-meaning people who want to "prove" that healing is not possible are *not* the ones we need to try to heal. When they come to a place where they are ready to surrender into the *possibility* that healing naturally is attainable, we may then help them. I never said it was easy. But it's simple. And it's *possible*. It's often tempting to preach from an inexperienced platform, but I eradicated that option. I now have the ability to speak from a real-life platform that matches the things I had previously only witnessed.

This is where my journey truly begins - the point of moving into my car and using three very powerful tools to heal and align with the life I came to live. Nature. Connection. Purpose.

And so I say to YOU, the reader whose eyes are looking at these words - YOU CAN HEAL. How badly do you want to?

Write your answer here to that question:

_____

When your answer is, "Enough to do whatever it takes," you're ready!

Let us embark on this spiritual journey together. I know it's "Julie's" spiritual journey that I embarked on, but the point of every blog I wrote was to awaken new ideas and possibilities for people. I wanted to write this book as a tangible piece of evidence that peace may be gained through a journey into spirit. And also as evidence that regardless of your level of depression, poverty, anger, or any negativity, you can choose to create your life as you wish.

My wish for you right now is to make the choice to believe it *will* get better and *you* have the power to make it so!

Do you make that commitment to yourself?

YES or NO? (Circle one.)

I also want to clarify that my intention, when sharing something painful or sharing details of a less-than-preferable situation, is only for the reader to connect to me in a human way, to relate to the depth of experiences and emotions we move through. If I pretend my life is nothing but perfect emotional balance, it would not be authentic to many of the experiences that made me who I am in this moment, writing to you.

Yes. YOU. One single person.

What's your name?

I'm writing to YOU!

But you'll also notice I don't stop at the pain. I've turned every experience into a powerful teaching opportunity and send gratitude out to each of these past moments. Perhaps you can come to the same place or already have.

From the inside out, I wish you an ever-expanding spiritual journey.

This book now departs from the day I moved into my truck and the blogs that came out of that experience. These blog entries have only been minimally edited. I wanted them to stay as raw and true to their original essence as possible. I hope the insights I gained and continue to gain touch some part of your heart, igniting the flame of all you came to share with this world. Thank you for taking this journey with me.

I'M HOME…(LESS)

Day 1 – August 14, 2014 – 8:47 p.m.

Yup! You read that correctly. I am technically homeless, but it feels more like "home" than "less". I drove through downtown Ventura today and watched all of the cracked-out-spewing-negativity-no-clue-where-they-are-filthy-from-head-to-toe-with-a-brown-bag-of-liquor folks. I feel no resonance with this energy despite our seemingly similar housing situation. I am, technically, living in my car (as of 9:00

a.m. this morning). However, I have many dear and sane friends; I take care of my personal hygiene, and I don't have an interest in sharing tales of woe and victimization (or partying them away). Although I left my house today, my sense of home is still with me. It feels like it's in the "cave of the heart" (as a dear friend describes to me often) and I can go there any time I choose. I can imagine some people would feel a bit of panic in leaving their home, but somehow the moment I stepped into my truck I felt free. A long breath left my chest and it was as if I knew something unbelievably good was around the corner. Happiness enveloped me. Not in any type of hokey way, but an authentic sense of joy and peace cradled me the very second I sat down for this next part of my journey.

Have more than a few seriously "hellacious" situations occurred in the last few years?

Certainly!

Have I lost jobs, failed at businesses, chose the "wrong" careers (We'll get to that later!), been devastated from loss of love, and watched people die or get horribly ill?

Certainly!

This is me the day I left my house, my cat, and my ex. This is posted so we can watch my face transition from pain to bliss along this spiritual journey.

22

But here's the *real deal*, folks – It's all my creation and it's all perfect, *and* it's allowing me to be right here, right now, blogging away and feeling more "on purpose" than I've ever felt before.

Regardless of where we lay our heads at night, we can empower ourselves. It doesn't mean I am superior to the dude in the park talking to the invisible rabbit about his fluorescent socks. It just means I recognize the power of my mind, my heart, and all that is. I can be, do, and have anything I want in the world. What I've wanted most in the last year or more, is to see the world, align with my purpose, connect with nature, be of service, and visit the people I cherish deeply! In a nutshell, I've turned this journey into an adventure and it's my hope that my blog, products, and services will truly help others come to that quiet place inside, knowing all is well. This quiet place can then be tapped to create the lives we desire for ourselves.

So who, specifically, is this blog (now book) for? Anyone who takes a gander at it is fine with me, but likely I will attract a very special group including free spirits, travelers, law-of-attractioners, new agers, nomads, pilgrims, people searching for their inner truth, spiritual philosophers, gay and transgender people, animal lovers, conservationists, writers, artists, families, givers, alternative therapists, healers, astrologers, teachers, etc. The point is, *everyone* is welcome here, but I likely will not attract a conservative crowd. This is a place we can speak freely and fearlessly about *anything*; therefore we will naturally attract open and conscious people who seek expansion versus control. I wish to attract those I can be of greatest service to by sharing my spiritual journey.

I'll be sharing stories, incredible people I meet, spiritual places I come across, viewpoints, insights, photos, videos, ethical businesses/products, ways to align with nature and your gifts, and much more. Most of all, I want to share how my spiritual journey unfolds, as all of this is coming from a place of total surrender. I'm not fighting my circumstances. I'm rolling downstream with them as the fabulous Abraham-Hicks team describes. At one point I realized how few people would trust themselves to make a Hyundai Tucson their home and head into the world with little to no plan. I, somehow, by the grace of God/Great Spirit/Creator, have been gifted with a sense of trust in the universe to support and carry me. Perhaps one of the main ways I may be of service is to help others do the same.

Tonight I am staying at my friend Gary's house. (Technically, I don't *need* to sleep in my car this evening.) He is away right now and I could not ask for a more peaceful home to rest my head. Gary is one of those friends I can tell virtually anything to. He's my ultimate "book geek" friend, and he is remarkably clean and organized – to the point I feel a sense of reverence the moment I enter his space. Everything carries an intention here. There are no piles of useless crap lying around. I tend to pile up papers, books, dust, and treasures from the sea with a side of lucky pennies, crystals, and "to do" post-its. It's a nice change to be here, to say the least!

Gary laminates great quotes and places them in great places, because he's a great person.

I promise I'll share more of my story, "how" I got here, the emotional spectrum I've been through, and much more. I just wanted to give you an immediate inside look into what my first day as a home...(less) person on a spiritual journey was like.

I tend to be goofy, make up my own words, throw in quippy random thoughts, and can get a bit long-winded. However, I channel everything straight through me with little censoring or editing. I hear (or rather feel) entire blocks of thought, as Esther Hicks describes when she channels Abraham. But I promise to give you my pure truth so that you will perhaps be inspired to live yours.

Here's to nature, connection, and aligning with your purpose. You are deeply loved and I am so grateful to be here with you right now.

(At the end of each blog I will post current books I am reading, movies, quotes, oracle cards I pick, inspirational videos, music, and more!)

Current book – *Among the Islands: Adventures in the Pacific* by Tim Flannery
Quote of the day – "I stood in the dark and listened. It was a fabulous night, moonless, warm and humid, with a hum of insects all around." – Tim Flannery

Where have you stood and listened to the night?

Wishing you an ever-expanding spiritual journey,

Julie xo

BACON AND HALF & HALF

Day 2 – August 15, 2014 – 7:49 p.m.

Morning view from Gary's house. Not too shabby!

With a blog title like that, how could this *not* be interesting?

I woke up bright and early this morning with a gentle fog slowly easing its way back to sea. I headed over to Arroyo Verde Park for a short hike. My body has been craving physical activity, pure water, and healthy food after many months of a fairly toxic diet.

To say I haven't been kind to my physical temple is an understatement. I've put on about fifty pounds in the last year or two due to one thing – stress! (Not that weight happens passively...what we put in our bodies is 100% an active participatory choice.) I can remember my family using food as an emotional band-aid throughout my life. For whatever reason, when I give up that free and wild part of myself, I instantly start dreaming of lox and bagels, pizza, and dark chocolate. Most of the people I know do this and repeat a vicious cycle of feel good and eat well, feel bad and eat poorly, feel good and eat well, feel bad and...(on and on).

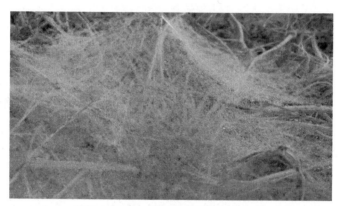

Incredible dew-drenched spider web on the trail.

Instead of using food as medicine, we use food as medication. *Big* difference! Medication relieves symptoms but typically cures nothing. Medicine balances, rejuvenates, heals, releases, brings up, dissolves, penetrates, and so much more!

Trail view – Arroyo Verde Park

I know part of my spiritual journey is to learn to love myself so divinely (including physically), it's natural for me to choose healthful food and physical exercise on an automatic basis. People do not lose weight and then get happy (although every magazine and commercial would have you believe this). They get happy; then they begin to lose weight, thinking it was the "diet" (when it was actually the self-love and happiness that instigated this).

We can't make an empowered choice from disempowered emotions such as despair, self-loathing, depression, or disgust. We must see the worth we have right this very minute – cellulite, pimples, wrinkles, and all! *Then* we may begin to shift our choices that flow from a sense of self-love. After all, we are spiritual beings living a physical experience. When the personal spiritual truth is aligned in us, the physical will follow.

The power of synchronicity is part of what becomes more and more noticeable as I've embarked upon this spiritual journey. This is where the "Bacon and Half & Half" story comes in (Be patient with me; everything above ties in beautifully!). As I hiked this morning, I came across three fat basset hounds with their human mom. She was the sort of dog owner who walks her dogs for the sole purpose of getting attention. The moment anyone makes eye contact with the dogs, she breaks into a story about how they woke up, dragged water across the floor, went outside for "poopie time", and which one went to the vet this week.

(All I did was look at the dogs.)

It only took a few seconds before all of the fat doggie names were relayed to me and I gave little Angela Basset (not kidding) a quick pet and booked it for the hills. I love, love, love animals but I don't need a sermon or seven page discourse on what's for breakfast in Doggieville.

Now – surely by no "accident" – on the way back to my car I chose the route that took me through the park instead of retracing my trail steps. Sure enough, I walked right past Ms. Basset Hound and her three princesses. She locked eyes on me like a wolf who just spotted a rabbit.

I could hear her thoughts. "You! You! The one who knows my doggies. Get over here right now and let me tell you what my dogs will eat for dinner!"

I looked away.

She kept staring and moved toward me.

I looked away harder.

Escaping by just a few feet, I saw her latch onto the park attendant and launch mid-sentence into a conversation, as if she knew him for years.

She started, "...that's why Suzie puts the bowl behind the door or else her food would be everywhere."

And the attendant replies, "Who's Suzie?"

She replies, "Well, the one feeding the doggies, silly!"

Of course! (Wait. It gets better.)

I hear distant utterances of her having to go home now to get their bacon.

She exclaimed, "It's bacon for breakfast! And if Angela won't eat it, I just pour half & half over it."

Did I book it the heck 'outta there'?

Heck yes I did!

No wonder those bassets were eight tons each. This was horribly unhealthy for the dogs. Before I could launch into my opinions about how unfit she was to own these dogs, I put my head down and reeled in the line that was ready to spew forth from my mouth.

I asked myself, "Julie, why did you run into that? You're on a spiritual journey. What on God's green earth was all that about?"

Then it hit me. How can I possibly judge the dog lady when I've been treating myself no different? Maybe breakfast isn't a bunch of bacon bits drowning in cream, but I've done some serious damage. (Any readers out there ever pass out in a bowl of pure whipping cream over Lucky Charms? Just asking. No judgment please. Ha!)

Part of a spiritual journey *is* a physical journey. To revere and honor the physical temple is to revere and honor whatever created it. I always feel more connected to Source/Spirit when I eat well and with consciousness. Spirit has a natural, inherent flow and when I block it, I feel energetically blocked as well.

This brings me back to my original idea about synchronicity. If I had picked any other trail or way back to my car, I never would have experienced the dog lady or reflected on my own health. If we begin following the path that feels good, many unforeseen experiences and realizations appear (of course, we have to be open to them).

I didn't think I'd be blogging on day two about my health challenges and weight gain. It's one of those things I'd rather sweep under the rug, pretend it didn't happen, avoid seeing people who know me as the raw food and health advocate, etc. But if we don't shine light on the dark places, they lurk there, forever unseen and therefore forever unreleased or unhealed. Once we shine the light, we need to love that dark place. My friend Randee always kisses herself. Yes, she actually kisses her hands and arms while she repeats, "I love you!"

We always have options. Choose intuitively and see what appears!

Tonight is an opportunity to kiss and unconditionally love this physical body I've been given. I'm going to make better choices about my food, my fitness, and how I view myself. Why? Because I'm pretty darn valuable and pretty darn awesome and pretty darn pretty. And so are YOU!

Current book – Still reading *Among the Islands* by Tim Flannery
Quote of the day – "Ladybugs are real good and very nice." – My brother, Zachary, age 4.

"BLESSED" BY A SEAGULL

Day 5 – August 18, 2014 – 4:18 p.m.

An old wives' tale claims it's good luck to be pooped on by a seagull. I always wondered where this tale came from. Today I am wondering even more, as a huge seagull flew over me, leaving me with a gift that ran down my arm and onto my shoe. Apparently there are some ties to Greek blessings. One Greek tale describes how great wealth will be coming to me should a seagull drop its "treasures" on my head. There are also some modern day stories that speak of chance. If I am lucky enough to get crapped on by a random seagull passing by (an extreme rarity), surely I am lucky enough to win the lottery. Well, I'm going to opt-in to my Greek roots.

"Listen up, Seagull Goddesses. Mama needs some gas money, so keep the gifts-a-comin'!"

This brings me to a memory of being in Brighton, England during college. I had just stored my backpack at the bus station and while walking around, a seagull pooped above me. I had poop running down my hair and all over my jacket. With no supplies to wash up, I walked back to the hostel I just checked out of and begged the attendant to loan me a towel and shampoo. It was also a Sunday and nothing was open for me to even see how horrible the damage was. Luckily my shampoo angel came through.

Anypoo, moving right along. It's been a really fun few days. I left the comforts of Gary's house in Ventura and headed up to Lake Piru. My dear friend Randee is house sitting on a friend's farm and I came to help out. Phew! Five goats, one donkey, two dogs, several chickens, and a cat will tire a gal out. But I love them all; they are hilarious! Animals truly make my heart dance.

I love the evenings up here. The breezes slow down and the coyotes come out hollering with fresh kills every night. My first night here I woke up somewhere between one and four a.m. I heard what sounded like a huge sonic boom, or what one would imagine a giant metal ball falling onto cement sounds like. But there are no mines and no airfields here. Just a quiet little river gorge.

Randee getting her "farm on".

All over the world, people are hearing this sort of "boom" with no explanation of what it is. Maybe gases exploding from the earth (We

are on sulfur hills here, so maybe Mama Earth has indigestion?).
Maybe plates are shifting. Who knows? I just know it sounded like it
was in the atmosphere as if something dropped to earth with a huge
thud. It was so intense I lifted my head and virtually felt my heart leap
out of my chest.

The spiritual and U.F.O. communities are trying to figure these sounds
out as well, but so far there are no absolutes. It's just amazing to
observe how much more "in tune" I feel and how much more I am
observing/experiencing when close to nature. In addition to the
unexplained sounds and good "luck" lately, I'm blessed with animal
love all around. Not only with the farm animals, but I've also seen
quail, crows, herons, hummingbirds, butterflies, a roadrunner, and
what I think was a rose breasted finch.

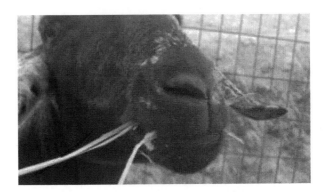

The quiet and peace here align me with my inner authentic voice. As
soon as I go to the city and all of the white noise crowds my brain, I
begin losing sight of things that are important to me and tend to hop
on the internet or watch movies to drown out the noise.

You can see in the photo below it's merely been a few days and
already my face is looking more clear and relaxed when you compare it
with the photo in my first blog entry.

I notice my senses coming alive as well. For example, I walked down to the Sespe Creek yesterday where the dam begins releasing water. The dragonflies were making love, the water was sounding happy, and as I rounded the corner I heard a huffing sound. I second guessed my ears, kept walking, and heard it again. My guess would be it was a bear or a mountain lion (both of which make such noises). I backed away and the hair on my skin started to rise as if I entered an electric field. I had nothing with me but water, so I knew better than to push on.

This connection with my senses always makes me feel so alive and present! Was I worrying about bills, jobs, or family issues? No way! I was alone, alive, filled up with alertness and being kissed by a baking-hot morning sun!

Speaking of the sun, I listen to people complain lately about the heat. But they moved to California to not have to deal with the snow. If people noticed how many times in just one week they complained about the heat, they may faint from "complaint exhaustion" instead of "heat exhaustion".

What are we energetically putting "out there" when we complain? We are, in essence, asking for more of what we don't want. The universe hears, "...heat, heat, hot, too hot, smoldering, skin burning,...". Well, get ready for more! How about, "I am so blessed and grateful I won't freeze today. I am so excited about this opportunity to get a suntan! I love how the sun helps my garden grow! I know nature will balance this heat with a wet and cool winter!"

On that note, it is almost time to feed the pups and water the garden. I'm grateful for the realizations that made their way home today. Nature is a must. Animals are a must. Trails are a must. Quiet time is a must. The musts are very clear, burning themselves into each cell and summoning the truth I came to live.

I truly love my life...even the seagull blessings.

Current book – *Loving what Is* by Byron Katie
Quote of the day – "Eventually you come to see that everything outside you is a reflection of your own thinking. You are the storyteller, the projector of all the stories, and the world is the projected image of your thoughts." – Byron Katie

POOP, PAWS, AND SWEET LIBERATION

Day 7 – August 20, 2014 – 6:09 p.m.

I thought about splitting this long blog into several. But I like the vastness of what I do in a day. It speaks to the variety of experiences I have when I'm surrendered to this spiritual journey-by -car!

Yesterday I left the farm animals and ventured back to Ojai. I arrived at Randee's studio (she stayed on the farm to finish out her work) that sits above the orange groves and looks over the Topa Topa mountains. "Stunning" is not a strong enough word to describe the view. I spent many Monday evenings in meditation here as Randee took us into a deep, sacred inner silence.

Earlier today I stopped at a honey farm/tasting paradise near Fillmore. I picked up some raw honey with cinnamon. This will be fabulous in tea (or in heaping spoonfuls mixed into nothing but my belly). Honey, from what I've researched, is the only food on the planet that never expires. Tombs thousands of years old contained perfectly preserved pots of honey that's still edible. Talk about a powerful spiritual food! I do feel a sense of elation when I eat honey. Most spiritual groups through history, at bare minimum, mention the magic or healing powers of honey. The key is to find 100% organic, raw, unfiltered types that also do not spray the bees with any toxic chemicals to sedate them. Honey can be harvested gently while the bees are mostly at rest.

Truly raw, unfiltered honey is cloudy in appearance and often solid at room temperature. It also does not give a burning sensation to the tongue like overly-sweetened "honey" that is often cut with corn syrup or other cooked, concentrated sweeteners. The average palette can handle a spoon of honey without feeling ill (most supermarket honey gives me a headache after the first bite). I've had many inner battles over the years about the ethics of honey harvest. Sometimes I feel okay about it, other times I feel sad for taking the honey, as the bees use it for food stores during the winter. I try to stay close to my gut and when it says not to eat honey, I don't. I believe we should call companies and empower ourselves to find places that leave some honey for the bees during winter and that practice ethical honey harvest. We need the bees. Bees are love and work for us to be able to eat the rest of the food that needs pollination for harvest.

In addition to my honey adventures, I've enjoyed some fun synchronicities today. I pulled the Chameleon card from my animal tarot deck, which represents "news of changing environment." Yesterday I also picked the "vacation" card and the "new location" card from my fairy oracle deck. Part of my spiritual practice involves centering myself in the morning and tuning in to what the universe wants me focused on. I know there was no accident I kept pulling cards about pets on the farm the other day. The cards about location I pulled are also lining up perfectly.

Minutes ago my friend Gary called offering me his place again while he is away. I've been feeling much like a chameleon as I shift through various homes and honor the way of living in each space. It's been interesting to see how people exist in their spaces as well. Each one is vastly different. The cards I pull continue to mirror my situations, feelings, and ways of moving through the world. I'll share more along my journey.

Back to my adventures! I hiked Horn Canyon Trail up to my favorite water hole this morning, but it was dry. The drought is pretty intense here currently, but I always remain trusting in the power of Mama Nature to bring balance when needed. I believe as we balance our own consciousness, we will see less extremes in the reflections around us.

I approached a little trickle of water and saw some of the largest animal prints ever in Ojai. Lately we've had bears and mountain lions coming to town in search of water, so it's no surprise their paw prints are nonchalantly descending the trail along with mine.

The amount of animal poop *on* the trail (not to the side of it) was like nothing I had ever seen. Giant piles, pellets with seeds and grass, twisted intestinal molds, and....oh my! At one point I came across a huge pile of excrement that included an entire plastic bag. It was twisted and slightly mixed into the poop. It must have been from a large mammal. It hurt my belly a little to think of all the plastic bags making their way onto trails and into the stomachs of these beautiful creatures. This is a good reminder for me to lessen my use of them as much as possible. I'm the gal who forgets her reusable bags and ends up carrying her groceries out in her arms to avoid bags. Ha!

In all seriousness, my trail journey today was a magical experience. I felt my heart pump, my sweat drip, and my nose come alive with the scent of sage and unknown herbs. Nature is my bliss. It's where I feel most connected to the spirit, or essence within. Part of what I came to teach people, is how to connect with spirit by being truly present in nature. I've never met a balanced person who was disconnected from the earth. Never. And that, too, will be expanded upon in the future.

The sun is now setting over the Topa Topa mountains. It's been a gorgeous day. I even had some time to visit with my dear friends Joyce and Gerry. They own a frame shop in town. Joyce is a gifted spiritual artist and Gerry is a gifted writer. I don't yet know much about his books but he gave me *The Road to Shambhala* today and so far it's a spiritual novel. I read three pages and was immediately sucked in. I highly recommend you check his books out and Joyce's artwork at www.joycehuntingtonart.com. I'm so grateful for these friends I can speak in depth with, ultimately raising our consciousness and connection.

In closing, I must share a Maya Angelou video I came across today called "Love Liberates". It was all about how authentic love sets a person free versus attaching to and boxing it in. She speaks of how her mother set her free to be who she is and focused on the good in her, regardless of how many times she came crawling back home. And when her mother passed, Maya liberated her by giving her permission to go (she lay dying of cancer). It was a truly magnificent video. It made me think of so many different loves I have had in this lifetime, platonic and otherwise.

You can watch Maya Angelou's video by searching "Love Liberates" on YouTube.

Part of why I am on this spiritual journey alone is my partner and I split up a while back. I will go into that a bit more in the future, but for now I'd like to share that by setting her free to do some necessary healing, I liberated myself simultaneously. I had lost the self-love that once seemed to come effortlessly and needed the space and freedom to fly again. I was lost in her healing process and forgot about my own needs. I know it's very painful for her to have been set free, but one day I hope she feels I've liberated her so she may blossom into the flower she keeps tucked away. I felt one of my own petals bust loose today and for that I say, "Love liberates!"

Current book – *Loving What Is* by Byron Katie
Quote of the Day– "Love liberates. It doesn't hold. That's ego. It libertates!" – Maya Angelou

ORACLES AND SYNCRONICITY

Day 8 – August 21, 2014 – 9:26 a.m.

Can you feel the faeries?

"Spiritual journey" is a fairly broad concept. It's different for everyone. Some people link religious journeys with spiritual journeys. Other people simply feel a spiritual journey is something that brings us closer to Source. Most of the people I've researched who claimed to be on spiritual journeys had, soon before embarking, lost a part of themselves and committed to re-awakening the most divine, authentic person they could. One could argue that every moment of every person's life is part of a spiritual journey and I would agree on some level. My own spiritual journey began with a decision to awaken the spirit within, the heart energy, and live through that (versus the mind and external influences) so that I may be of service using the gifts I came here to use.

Many spiritual journeys involve a deeper awareness of the coincidences that seem to magically appear. As we choose to be more in tune with our inner experiences and guidance system, the external world becomes a beautiful reflection of that. It's not necessarily that there were no synchronicities or happy accidents before we chose to step into a deeper sense of spirit; it's perhaps that we become more conscious or open to the magic. Today was a perfect example of that.

I don't "need" oracle or tarot cards, crystals, or anything else to be able to get through my day. They're tools I choose to use and they often help align me with a specific energy. They're also helpful when I need centering (like when my mind runs amuck). Yesterday, for example, I pulled a number of cards that seemed to attract events of similar vibration almost instantly.

First, I kept pulling the card "share" from my unicorn oracle deck. I was feeling the experience of not having much to share with people right now (nothing monetary anyway), but used this as an opportunity to see what I did have to give. Shortly after, my friend Gary called to say he had to leave town right away and that I could have all of his organic farmer's market greens. I could have hoarded them all, especially since I had little to no money to buy quality food, but I chose to give some to my dear friend Jo who loves to juice. Some of the greens also went to one of my spiritual teachers, Lokpal. He loves greens!

How fabulous it felt to be overflowing in vegetable abundance and then to spread that "wealth" to others in the middle of financial poverty! The point here is not to give me a pat on the back, but to pay attention to the synchronicities at hand. It was my choice to get in touch with the vibration of sharing and the universe therefore answered and provided. I could have ignored the oracle card, thinking it was silly that I had anything to share with my loved ones.

I've also noticed many red-tailed hawks and other birds flying overhead. I hiked the new botanic garden trail in Ventura yesterday and a giant hawk flew right over my face, landed on a tree next to me, and watched me as I whistled. Hawks represent "guardianship in ventures" which makes sense given I am starting this new blog/book. I feel I must protect my venture as if it's a sacred child, my gift to the world. I feel this in my soul. It's like a deep, sacred excitement about what I can give birth to and share with you!

"Grandparent" was the other card I pulled yesterday and had been talking at length with my friend about my grandmother who passed years ago. I believe she is one of my guides now and I hope to see her in spirit one day.

After my hike I walked to the gorgeous neo-classical City Hall to check out the marble walls, artwork, etc. My dad called while there and told me my grandfather, Al, can never swallow again and had to decide between dying or using a feeding tube. Heart-wrenching! This is a man who loved food (in a very obsessive way) and had been on the brink of death for ten years. I was told he initially he chose to die and likely his kids or wife convinced him otherwise, as he suddenly chose the tube. I have not heard about my PaPa Al in months, yet I pulled a card about the unbreakable bond of a grandparent and within hours I receive a call about him.

So what's the point?

Are you paying attention to the miracles and synchronicities all around you?

Pay attention, tune in, and feel something before it happens. I chose to align with the oracle card energies of sharing and connecting with my grandparents. It literally was handed to me on an appetizer platter within hours.

We can create our synchronicities and coincidences. In fact, we're never not creating them because we are always attracting things based on our feelings (or vibrations). Isn't that empowering? I feel like a magician when I really take that in!

Everything is connected in this beautiful spiral of life...

What can you align with and create today? Do you have an oracle or tarot deck? Start simple. Use a tool to help you focus and watch what happens in your life! Keep feeling into what you're focused on. It's not about the things you want to attract, it's about the feelings you will have when they come in. A great book that might help you understand this on a deeper level is *Ask and it is Given* by Esther and Jerry Hicks. I'll expand more on this topic in future blogs. For now, begin to open up to more synchronicity in your life and it can truly guide you along the way!

Current book – *Loving What Is* by Byron Katie
Quote of the day – "Would you rather be right or free?" – Byron Katie

LIKE WHITE ON RICE

Day 10 – August 23, 2014 – 7:37 p.m.

Is this really the tenth day of my home(less) experience?

Yes. Yes it is.

I'm sitting at a camp I worked at all summer. There's an event here tonight and a gal referred me to watch a few infants while the parents party it up. Essentially, I stare at a baby monitor to see if the kids crank at all late at night and get paid to do it.

Money comes to me like white on rice these days. Little money-making projects come to me effortlessly. That doesn't mean I don't put in effort where it's needed. If someone calls, I call back. If an opportunity presents itself, I explore it. I am not, however, focusing my efforts on "finding" a job I don't want and entering into the panic vibration most broke people take on. (This is *key*. If you feel panicked about money or jobs, consider reading that statement again.)

I have one more check on its way from my summer camp job. In the meantime, every penny I need shows up. Babysitting, delivering magazines for a company I worked for, intuitive readings for a gal who's been calling me over the last few years. When I'm in the flow of feeling good and connecting to spirit, I don't have to "think" or "plan" my way into what I'm supposed to do. I stay open and humble, and opportunities present themselves. My gut says "yes" to some opportunities and clearly says "no" to others. I trust the response and this is one of the key things I am learning. Part of the reason I am in this predicament is because I stepped away from my gut to take on potential opportunities that didn't settle right, but I thought I would make a lot of money doing them. Isn't that interesting? We are taught to go after good jobs, good money-making opportunities with strong histories of success; but we are not taught to listen to the voice within that says, "I am not interested in doing this for a living," or "This person has a strange vibe. I should keep looking."

When a person doesn't have a "good job", people wonder what the hell is wrong with him or her. Their assumption is that the person is an idiot who must not *want* a good job. Of course everyone wants a good job (whether that's working for oneself or not), but that term is different for everyone. The mainstream definition of that good job includes the ability to pay your bills with leftover savings, having benefits, retirement, and the company needs to be stable or thriving. The definition of a good job for a free spirit with the heart of an entrepreneur includes the following:
- Provides the income to do whatever I choose (with the understanding this may take some time).
- Benefits are irrelevant because I have enough abundance to do as I please and pay for everything with cash; nor do I encourage

or support the current benefit system designed to disempower people and induce fear.

- I am treated with respect and treat others with respect.
- I can speak openly without being fired, belittled, bullied, shamed, or controlled.
- I work with a team of people who are open, communicative, and want the best for everyone.
- The business does good for humanity and the planet.
- The business operates on a system of integrity and fairness.
- An understanding of time with family and nature is valued and encouraged versus working overtime.
- Etc. This is the tip of the iceberg!

Great seeds exist within us. Just breathe and tune in to what wants to be sowed.

Here's the dealy-o. I'm not trying *not* to get a job. I'm open to it. So far I've been needed various places doing little things here and there. I'm also dedicating time to building my website (preparing for my future), blogging, and honing in on my vision. Not to mention, I've been exhausted and emotionally bruised up from the recent break-up, having to leave my cat to a foster home for a while until my ex has a new place, and facing major financial challenges. This time of freedom, though it appears I am just a broke gal with no job living in her car, has been *essential* for getting back in touch with my joy, nature, books, my health, and the authentic me. I was given the opportunity to either choose to surrender or go into the panic we are taught to have as soon as we don't have a "good job".

Where does this panic come from?

Obviously, we are handed down our beliefs from generation to generation (the point here is not to rip apart the wrong-doings of our past generations, but to look at them honestly and find the places we can make better or more empowered choices). Most of my family (but not all) considered it a "shame" when someone gets fired or laid off. Pay attention to the language your mentors and society used growing up. "Isn't it a shame she's out on the street? What a horror Bobby lost his job. That's just terrible that she can't pay her bills! Having that much debt is just regrettable."

No big deal? Or do we end up wired with these negative feelings, further berating ourselves when we end up in similar predicaments?

For whatever reason, as I grew up I never resonated with the horror. I *always* had the sense that all was well and always would be well, that every job lost is a job gained with more potential for growth, appreciation, and abundance. Doors close. People forget that doors also open. They just stare at the door that closed and say, "What a waste. What a shame. This is awful. You're whole education was a waste! What now? I didn't deserve to have you fall short."

Here's the whole point – I refuse to panic because all is well and I feel flippin' fabulous!

Sit quietly for a moment if you've just lost your job, your spouse did, you claimed bankruptcy, or you perhaps had to downsize drastically. Can you hear your heartbeat? Has that changed within the "job-having" you to the "job-lacking" you?

You see, all is well. You're breathing, reading this blog on a high-tech device (or paper) and likely opening to your own spiritual journey. What more do you need in this moment?

In a new moment, life will bring you those new moment needs. It can't not come to you. It's like white on rice. Doesn't that feel better than the panic? (If you know someone who may be experiencing lack, please purchase this book for them. You may just create a smile today and a whole lot of relief!)

Current book – *Hero* by Rhonda Byrne
Quote of the day – "The effect naysayers have is up to you. Only you choose how you react to them." – Rhonda Byrne

DOG DROOL AND HUMAN DROOL

Day 13 – August 26, 2014 – 9:00 p.m.

A German shepherd just deposited a drool-soaked tennis ball on my journal. This has been occurring every few minutes as I (attempt to) write.

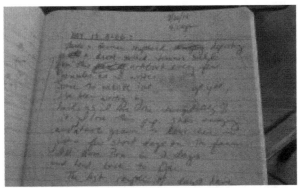

Notice the dog drool and mud from the tennis ball. I wasn't kidding!

My website is not live yet, so I have been writing by hand. I love the tangibility of it. I also love this pup I'm staying with. She's amazing. Isn't it wild that I have grown to love her in just a few short days on the farm? (I returned to help Randee some more with the animals.) I'll leave this land in two days and head back to Ojai.

The last couple of days have been wonderful, to say the least; drool-worthy, actually. I felt a huge release of anger toward my ex-girlfriend after a peaceful e-mail exchange. I know love is the only real deal. Everything else is simply mind chatter.

Large amounts of my time are spent at the stream and also at a secret pool of water I found below the dam. It is not visible from any streets, or even from any main trails. I took a side trail the other day and almost passed out when I saw the first green pond, stocked full of steelhead trout. One was at least sixteen inches. Further up the trail I happened upon a magic faerie pond with greens and browns set against a bright blue sky, with a canyon cathedral around one side. Instantly I notice there was no graffiti, no trash, and no evidence of humans! That was the best part. There were paw prints everywhere. Coyotes and deer definitely frequented the area. I saw one big buck make his way down to the water the other night.

The depth of nature I've experienced lately has been healing me from the inside out. Most people (it seems), when faced with being homeless, are on the prowl to change the situation. I feel none of this. I feel exactly on path and on purpose. I feel deeply connected to Source/Spirit/Nature. I feel a renewed sense of love and respect for myself. I feel brave. I feel adventurous. I feel present in my heart. I feel gratitude. I feel abundance. I feel like serving others from the heart. I feel loving and loved.

When I wrote in the last blog about money coming to me with ease, from a place of surrender, I was not joking on any level. The people I will cat sit for in September offered me money to take them to the airport and pick them up upon their return. Then my mom randomly sent me a VISA gift card she did not need with fifty bucks on it. And I might be able to housesit for dear friends of mine soon if they can get away. Opportunities come to me when I am in the flow!

Today was the first day in a very long time when I did not feel a single thing in my life needed to change. I was in total peace and clarity. I told my friend Randee this and we both felt so good. What a gift! Some people never feel that, not even for a single moment. People are perpetually on a merry-go-round of wanting what's around the next bend instead of noticing the beauty they are sitting on.

Last night Randee brought me a fortune cookie. The fortune said, "Success will be yours." What are the chances of that timing? I knew in the moment that I was already successful, that what I felt today was a gift beyond what most people achieve in a lifetime. Pure, present, peace.

It's been a gorgeous evening. My big shepherd friend is tuckered out and the chunky chihuahua is cuddled by my side waiting for his bed. Am I blessed or what? Indeed, I'm a blessed and drooling nature-soaked animal fiend.

Got snacks?

Current book – *Theodosia – The Flower Wizard of California* (Oh my lord this book is so awesome!) by Myrtle Shepard Francis
Quote of the day – "To know and not to do is not to know." – Leo Buscalia (via Wang Ming who lived from 1472-1529) Steven Covey also said similar. There are various opinions out there on quote ownership.
Oracle Card – Yesterday I pulled the "Listen to your feelings" card for the fifth time in a row. I even pulled it a few times in one day! And thus I have been listening.

HOMELESSNESS IS OFTEN WEIRD

Day 19 – September 1, 2014 – 7:57 p.m.

Last night, technically, was the first night I spent in my truck. I could have called a friend, but I had already enjoyed eighteen nights at the homes of friends and people who left town and offered their places. Last night was interesting (well, let's call it weird), to say the least!

First, I drove up to Potrero John Trail outside Ojai in the wee hours of morning. Knowing my car would sizzle while I hiked, I dropped off my sensitive articles at storage. No one likes deep roasted computer or sun baked credit cards after a long hike. It was a strange feeling to have to plan where to put my belongings just to enjoy a hike on a hot summer day (Ojai often hovers around 100-110 degrees this time of year).

Another let's-just-say-odd experience was returning to my car when I was full of dust, sweat, and trail "decorations" such as thorns, rosehip pieces, and clingy unidentifiable plant parts. I know. You're probably thinking this is no biggie. But I had no shower nearby and my fresh clothing was buried under piles of stuff in the car. (At some point it becomes an art to unravel your belongings and properly pack them for accessibility. Obviously, I was clueless about this or would have put my clothing somewhere attainable in the moment).

I took off with my "stank" and headed back to town. Don't get me wrong. I'm not complaining. I'm merely pointing out the little things we take for granted such as a hot shower post-hike and a desk to safely keep a computer from being sun-charred. The day was young and I had the odd sensation of not having anywhere to be. I could have done some work at the coffee house, but chose to wander a bit.

My parking spots were chosen on the basis of shade availability, as my computer was retrieved from storage by this point. I parked in an empty lot by the Ventura River Preserve where I'd hiked many times. There was one oak tree I backed under and read for a while. My front windows were down which allowed a rush of splendid canyon wind to pass through. At one point a turkey buzzard and a red-tailed hawk flew directly behind my car, landed to fight over a carcass, and flew around the car for a few minutes. I had been so quiet while I read they must not have noticed me. It was remarkable to watch them in my rear-view mirror.

Moments like these instantly connect me with Source. How many people are gifted with seeing a close-up of something like this? I didn't see this while home on the computer. I saw this only because I chose to quietly sit in nature, read, surrender, and allow the "need" to be busy "doing" something fall away. The universe always responds with greatness when I surrender like this.

I wanted to sprawl out a bit so I left for a sunset at Sarzotti Park. What a strange experience to have lived two blocks away in a cute little house and then to have sprawled out on a blanket with no home to walk back to. I watched a couple of drug addicts ride their bikes across the grass, swearing at each other and eagerly setting up to party. Although I knew I too was homeless in that moment, I felt completely removed from their vibe. My insides were swelling with feelings of abundance and amazement at the beautiful, sun-kissed grass.

The sun continued to set and I realized I had to use the restroom...badly! It was Labor Day weekend and all of the restrooms I visited were filthy. Again, I could have called a friend but felt I needed to experience all of this and do my best through it. It's difficult to fear what we've overcome, so in that regard I felt like I was overcoming something I used to fear (not having a restroom available).

I drove around for at least thirty minutes, carefully choosing a spot to park my car for the night. This is another weird aspect of my first night in my car (I didn't realize it would take so much work to park somewhere). I had the inner sense that the place I parked needed to meet the following criteria:

- Dark enough to sleep without headlights in my face
- A place the cops would not likely check out
- A quiet area
- A safe neighborhood
- A place I could move around in the car without people seeing me

The spot I chose was on a dark corner in front of someone's backyard fence. Perfect. The occasional car would pass by, but as long as I left before sunrise, no one would ever know I was there.

Look at the pollen it's collected! So cool!

Changing clothes was not easy. My trunk was filled with stuff on one side and I slept on the other side. By the grace of God I slipped into some pajamas without too much commotion. After settling, I realized my teeth were not brushed, yet I had no energy at that point to brush them, which takes me to another weird thing. How does a person nonchalantly brush her teeth in the car? She doesn't. She has to spit all over the place, which is just not groovy, or she carries a jar to spit into and empties it frequently when near sinks. Yes, much better.

I heard a few folks stroll by early in the night but mostly it was quiet. I woke several times. The need to pee was intense, but I waited until 6:30 a.m. when I happily saw the neighborhood was still sleeping. I crawled out of my truck and left.

Potrero John Trail... entirely surrounded by thick scrub brush. I felt like mountain lion appetizer right here.

The whole experience was just plain odd! You would have to live that day to understand, but it was a blend of deep spiritual connection, the feeling of having nowhere to be, and the strain of finding both a clean restroom and a safe street to bunk down on. Not that Ojai isn't one of the safest places in America; I just didn't want to draw attention to myself unnecessarily.

Perhaps some of you have experienced some of what I've shared. Perhaps not. I find there are more people who relate to me than I would have initially assumed. And the main thing people relate to is the freedom I am living and their desire to do so in their own way one day. Here's to keeping things weird!

Current book – *Theodosia: The Flower Wizard of California* by Myrtle Shepard Francis
Quote of the day – "You have GREATNESS within you!" – Les Brown
Oracle Card (Doreen Virtue Unicorn deck) – Forgive. It's time to let go of anger or blame.

IT'S ONLY NOON FOR ONE MINUTE

Day 30 – September 12, 2014 – 11:06 p.m.

The last eleven days have been spent almost non-stop on this blog (book) and creating a written piece about quality of life. I'm feeling extremely productive. Currently, I'm watching an adorable cat, Maya, and house sitting for some new friends. We had a wonderful conversation on the way to the airport about books and spirituality. I was introduced to the book *The Pathway of Roses* by Christian Larson. Amazing! It gets a little wordy here and there, but so many passages resonate with me. There's nothing like a moment when we attract the next great book to drool over. My fellow book lovers out there will completely get that.

Maya the wonder cat. I plan on saturating this book with cuteness :-)

Today has been so incredible! A friend I met through a local healer stopped by for a couple of hours before we went to the Friday healing session. I keep attracting conscious people on this spiritual journey and it feels so wonderful. She and I had a great chat about masterminds,

Napoleon Hill, books, shamanism, and so much more. She is also launching a website soon which will reveal what she's practicing, spiritually. While my family knows I dabble in the spiritual arts, I don't think they know the depth to which my spiritual practice is important. My new friend and I discussed how many of the things we will write about on our sites will be likened to a foreign language to many of our family members. We also know our family loves us unconditionally; it's just interesting to observe when we transparently put who we are into public.

This launch feels a bit like being naked and strapped to a gynecologist chair. There is literally nothing that can be hidden when we make the choice to expose the truth of who we are. Imagine if we all did this! Imagine if just a small percentage of us did this! Imagine if you did this just a little bit more in your own life! How many people would be living their dreams instead of hiding behind an identity they *think* will comfort others?

So back to my friend and I. As we chatted today I received an instant download or "chunk of thought" that helped me understand why most people regularly seem challenged. (Why is this not the reverse? Why aren't we rarely challenged and only once in a blue moon something comes up to help us grow?)

Let us pause for cat paws.

Hopefully I can effectively describe this, as it came to me beyond verbiage-land. When the sun is directly above us, there is no shadow. This is our point of greatest luminosity, when the darkness is completely eradicated. How often does this happen in one day?

Just once.

It's only noon for one minute! (Technically, one billion quadrillion zillionth of a second, but let's go with the cup half full take on things.)

As the sun moves slightly, we begin to see our shadow (literally and figuratively). If we use this as a metaphor, it makes complete sense that we have brief spurts of glorious passion, momentum, clarity, emotional balance, insight, etc…. Everything else is an attempt to keep focused on the light versus the ever-present shadow. Our shadow is virtually always with us. Thus, we tend to perpetually experience shadows (or challenges) except during this brief moment at high noon. It's not that the sun has left us outside of noon, it's merely throwing shadows. How we respond to the shadows (or whether we focus on them) is key. The challenge is to constantly know the "truth" which is that the sun is ever-present. Shadows are the illusions of its absence, the darkness we can focus on or simply acknowledge and move past. We also cannot "outwalk" our shadow, pretending it does not travel with us. It can, however, travel very matter-of-factly, embraced as one aspect of the self as we delve deeper into the light that always burns within.

By launching my website I am creating a journey into the light, regardless of the dark realities that exist (such as homelessness, lack of work, financial debt, overweight, emotional trauma from a break-up…). It's not that we have to ignore the shadows or pretend they are not there. But do they have to sabotage us until we choose suffering over bliss? Your shadow follows you everywhere, but it can never hurt you. If you *choose* to stare at your shadow all day, you'd likely get hit by a car, develop neck pain, or who knows what! Our point of focus is our choice. And it's also our choice in that split second of pure sunshine to ride the wave of light into divine bliss, pure shakti, creation, insight, whatever you like to call it!

I will ride the wave of that perfect noon-time moment, drenched in light, and charge my batteries so full there will always be enough light seeping its way into the shadows of my soul.

Try to handle it.

What needs illuminating in your life? I believe this is the most important question we can ask ourselves in this precious moment.

Current book – *The Pathway of Roses* by Christian Larson
Quote of the day – "When we begin to live for a great and good purpose, we place in action that law that causes all things to work

together for good. Henceforth, nothing is in vain; every person, thing, or event that comes into the world will add to the welfare, the richness and the beauty of that world. All living things become ministers of the life that is real life, we have been giving our best everywhere, and we are receiving the best from every source in return." – Christian Larson

See ya later... keep your eyes focused on the light!

DEATH, FREEDOM, AND THE GREATEST GRANDPA EVER

Day 34 – September 16, 2014 – 8:32 p.m.

Day 34. Interesting. Until I counted out the days to put the header on this blog, I had no idea it was the day of my lucky number "34". My grandfather, Pa Pa Al, passed away this morning at the age of 90. I've been told he passed peacefully with a smile on his face. This is the greatest of all blessings I could ask for.

PaPa Al in his waders. Classic.

He lived a difficult life, physically, over the last decade or more. At the end he could not speak; his lungs were full of liquid; he could no longer eat; and the hospital put a feeding tube in his stomach. This is no graceful way to live, so in the last couple of days, I sent messages to his higher self that it was okay to go. I also wanted to talk to him again, to tell him it's ok to leave, to let him know my Grandma Marge would wait for him on the other side, and so much more. But I'll settle for a peaceful passing over my own closure needs. There truly is only one great thing happening - love. And we can tap into that regardless of life or death, here or there, this or that.

PaPa Al and I after a grade school performance. His smile lit up the planet.

PaPa Al was a great man, literally. He was tall and robust, to say the least. Food was his greatest love outside of fishing and family. Pa Pa Al and Grandma Marge had an Airstream they built onto and turned into the "trailer". It was parked/built in the Upper Peninsula of Michigan in a town of approximately seven people. Ha! Maybe not seven, but the town was very small!

My childhood is rich with memories of berry picking, searching old buildings in the ghost town of Mandan, visiting Copper Harbor, eating pasties, fishing the most gorgeous streams imaginable, and much more. They also had a home in Chicago near Lake Michigan. My brother, Jonathan, and I would always go somewhere special with my grandparents like the Museum of Science and Industry, or to see plays such as *The Nutcracker*. They gave me exposure to art, music, abundance, nature, great films (My favorite was *Konrad* about a strange boy who was born in a factory but ended up being greatly loved.), and amazing food.

Pa Pa Al liked to suck the marrow out of chicken bones. Not kiddin'. It would take him hours to eat the spread Grandma Marge would leave trailing down the dining room table. Everything from bagels to truffles and Jewish brisket were traditional foods in their home. The aunts, uncles, and cousins would run the halls, laughing hysterically, and then take the eerie freight elevator down thirteen flights to the basement (They lived in a high-rise condo.). I have distant memories of dark corridors, a laundry room, a storage area with extra food and refrigeration, and the musty sound and smell of blended cultures. There was an essence of chicken noodle soup, Italian food, ice-cream, and mothballs everywhere. It's a smell I miss.

PaPa Al and Grandma Marge on their wedding day.<3

Today was strange. When my phone rang, I knew Pa Pa Al died. I let it go to voicemail because I had to keep it together and pick up the folks from the airport whose home and cat I was watching. I listened to the message after a short bit and my dad was sobbing. He had a stroke about two years ago and when he cries, sometimes he starts laughing.

It just happens. So he would cry and then chuckle. I did call him back on the way to the airport because I just had to. I couldn't wait. I cried immediately, uncontrollably. Today is also dad's wife, Cara's birthday, so it was bittersweet. And yesterday was my little cousin Matthew's tenth birthday, and he was deeply connected to his Great Grandpa. Such a beautiful bond. The first time they really communicated was when Matthew was about seven and PaPa Al could barely speak. When PaPa Al saw him, he began to cry. Matthew patted him on the back, held him, and told him "it's okay." I've never witnessed elsewhere the beauty and sensitivity this kid had with an older person, who looked kind of gaunt and scary. Matthew's wisdom helped him know the soul mattered most and the physical was irrelevant.

Today I posted a memorial to my PaPa Al on Facebook. That's strange in itself. My aunt, cousin, and I sent text messages but we did not talk on the phone. We enjoyed each other's posts on Facebook. But I had a deep yearning to be with them, to pull out old photos, tell stories, and remember the beauty of PaPa Al. This brought up a great frustration in me. The limitation poverty places on us seeps into every part of our lives. None of his kids have the money to come to Chicago from Michigan and throw a memorial right now. And I don't have money to go there or I would book a flight *tonight* and be there pronto. Yes, the connections on Facebook and texting were full of love, etc. But I missed the connection of hugs and family. I did see my friend, Jo, this morning and she is great support. She gave me big hugs that really helped and her husband had warm hugs and kind words as well.

This is part of what I want to show people on this spiritual journey. While no one can break the bonds of love we have with our families, it is certainly a break in the freedom flow when you cannot be with your loved ones. Being financially free *is* part of being fully free.

If a person lives off the grid, has all their friends and family local, and uses none of society's resources, that's a different story. Screw financial abundance, because they are growing and harvesting and building and have all they need. But when we make the choice to be "of this world" and work within its framework, we also make the choice to create whatever financial situation we choose.

For a long time I settled and chose to allow poverty to hold me back from many things. Life is a series of choices. I am choosing now to do more, create more, and do the best job I can at driving an income that will bring true freedom. The freedom of being able to truly connect with those I love, regardless of where they are; the type of income that will drive freedom to leave a legacy and resources to those who come after me; the type of freedom to choose my bliss rather than having my bliss chosen for me. If someone in your family has a reunion, invites you, and you can't go because of money, you are not free! But you can be. I believe in you. Sometimes we must acknowledge the reality before we create a new one. It is sobering, but necessary.

Right now I am not completely free and I desire greatly to be. I have freedom of time and space. I can go as I please down the street, I have no schedule, I have nowhere I am committed to be except a Thursday night mastermind and coaching meeting, a Friday healing session (by choice) and the rest is pure openness. I take work as it shows up; I work on my site and projects with a sense of excitement on a schedule I like. I work passionately when I work. But to be truly free, I must be financially free. Until then, I will feel a sense of abundance and freedom in order to bring it forward in a more concrete way.

The purpose of this discussion is not to make you feel disempowered or to feel you don't have everything you need within to make your dreams happen. Sometimes we just need to take a realistic inventory of our situation and make a decision to move toward true freedom rather than the illusion. I am taking ownership of creating my freedom. I have the freedom to choose if I want to enter into the monetary system or rebel against it. Therefore, I have to take what comes with it. And I am fine with that.

Sometimes all it takes is a view like this to feel free and abundant!

Anyway, it's with sadness in my puffy eyes (and happiness that my grandpa won't suffer) that I say goodnight and pack into my truck. I was craving the cool ocean air after our record 107 degree day in Ojai. I drove to the ocean tonight, said goodbye to my sweet Pa Pa Al on the waves as the sun set, and now type this blog at a coffee house. I will find a safe spot, crawl into my surprisingly comfortable sleeping "thingy-majingy", and call it a night.

Here's to the 34th blog, my 34th day home (less), and my Pa Pa Al, one of the truly great and loving beings of this dimension. He's in a new place now and I know he and Grandma Marge will visit me over the years.

Go find a trout, Pa Pa Al. And make sure it's a "lunker".

Song of the Day – *In the Lion* By Edward Sharpe and the Magnetic Zeros.
Here are the words to the video linked below:

Na na na na na na na but
I want to stay
I feel the love, I feel the love
I feel the love, I feel the love
Na na na na na na na but
I want to stay

In the lion, there's a heart breaking by the fire
And in the fire, there's a flame that wants to be the waterfall
In the water, there's a fishy swimming by the lovers
And in the lover, there's a tear that gonna be the inferno
In the lion, there's a heart breaking by the fire
But in the fire, there's a heat enough to cage around your soul

I feel the love, I feel the love, I feel the power
It's getting weirder by the hour
The world is fucked up but I want to stay

I feel the love, I feel the love, I feel the power
I'm tough enough to be a flower
The world is fucked up but I want to stay

This video may be found at:

https://www.youtube.com/watch?v=y98A7gUnOPk

Quote of the day – "When you speak, do not simply say words; say more. Never indulge in empty speech; that is, place yourself, your whole self, your great self into every word you utter. Let the spoken word be the body of your speech, but see that everybody has a great soul." – Christian Larson from *The Pathway of Roses*.

THE WINDS ARE-A-CHANGIN'

Day 37 – September 19, 2014 – 7:53 a.m.

I'm excited! The winds are-a-changin' as the old saying goes. While the last seven years have been full of change such as moving, job changes, and relationship shifts; a certain aspect of my life felt very stagnant or "stuck". The town of Ojai and its beach neighbor, Ventura, started to seem less than ideal. Until this week, they felt like safe, sleepy little towns full of abundance.

Beautiful Ventura, California

Last night was the third night in a row I slept in my car. Two nights were spent in the Ventura Harbor (I missed the permit-only sign the first night and the second night I didn't care because it felt safe.), and last night was spent near a state beach on a quiet street. As I drove around seeking spots to park the last few nights, there were several things I noticed:

- Ventura does not seem like the quiet beach town I once thought it was.

- There are *lots* of people who live in their vehicles, predominantly old, rusted-out vans with various accoutrements tied with bungee cords to anything that hangs off the vehicle.
- Homeless people have inundated virtually every crevice of Ventura. There are swarms of them on the pier, along the entire boardwalk, throughout every green area or park, and all over downtown and Main Street. I've heard L.A. drops them off up here when there are "too many" down there, but not sure if that is factual.
- Society does not make it easy for a homeless person to park and rest safely. Almost every street has signs such as, "No parking 2 a.m. - 5 a.m." Really? I have to wake up and move my car at 2 a.m.? There is almost nowhere that allows overnight parking except neighborhoods, but this presents a problem because I have to be sure no one sees me sleeping in my car or potentially calls the police.

Boardwalk trash on a typical day.

This morning I drove around for at least an hour looking for clean restrooms and a shower, as I hadn't showered since two nights ago at my friend's house. My hunt for showers resulted in findings of more change. These were things I did not ever notice, or pay attention to over the last few years:

- The entire Rincon and State Beach area is littered with masses of toilet paper (from people peeing and crapping by their cars when they visit the beach for the day). Beer cans, potato chip bags, and candy wrappers also litter the area.
- The parks that have showers now charge by the minute. Good to know, as I had no quarters with me and therefore could not bathe.
- There is graffiti virtually everywhere along the beach areas. I remember a little bit over the years, but most of where I stop to see the waves is tagged with various professions of love and salutes to hometown gangs.
- A toilet that flushes properly or that is not stuffed up is a rarity and also a treasure to behold like the Glory of God. No wonder they call it the Porcelain Throne; we should treat it as such, a rare royal specimen to treasure and lavish with appreciation!

I've noticed some of the same things in Ojai, a place that was incredibly clean and virtually devoid of litter seven years ago. My favorite place to pull off the road for a little streamside nap is now covered in graffiti marks. The trails I visit have more trash than ever before. More and more people are hanging shoes from wires throughout town (for those of you who are not "in the know", this can sometimes represent a street where a person can buy drugs). There are also loads of homeless people trailing around town. We always had a couple who might sleep at Libbey Park, but now there are homeless drug addicts in groups hanging out at the fountain behind our local shopping arcade, a few guys on bikes who get cans out of the recycle bins, and other interesting misfits and drifters.

One woman sleeps on Bryant street up against a nice office building and leaves before the business people show up. She's a loner, doesn't like to be looked at, and is extremely frail. Her hair has flat sides resembling clown hair on some days and other days she looks like she tried to clean up a little. If one looks closely, one can see the beauty she likely reflected years ago. I always wonder what her story is, and assume she chose Ojai because of its relative safety (in comparison with, let's say, almost every town in Los Angeles).

Sometimes ya gotta focus on the beauty amidst the filth.

There's also a person (I believe a lady) who sleeps in a white covered pick-up truck. It's so full of trash and hoarded "stuff", there likely is no room to lay down. She must sleep in the driver's seat, however I've never gotten close enough at night to see if this is the case. I wonder why people live in filth and piles of hoarded junk in a space that's so small. I have quite a few bags, a cooler, my business gear, and my sleeping pads. This feels extremely crunched even though it's all relatively organized. I can't imagine my car piled high with fast food wrappers and mail from twelve years ago. Compassion creeps in when I think about these people and their piles of junk.

Why is all of what I am noticing important? Because there is always a storm before the greatest blue skies imaginable. All of this change and toxicity in my environment is evidence that the world is on a precipice of massive change. We cannot move forward like this and survive. It's impossible. People are crapping in the waterways, running around in drug-induced stupors, littering the walkways out of pure laziness, and lacking the ambition to live their dreams. Part of me wants to run away to an even quieter town, an even sleepier town. But I know that just because I downsize from a town of 8,000 (Ojai) to a town of 100 does not guarantee a community of consciousness, cleanliness, or people living their dreams. The real mission is to change the inner self, which in turn begins to change the external experiences.

Ventura sunset

Most people would see these lists of negative qualities as something to get depressed about. I am choosing to use it as momentum to create more of what I want. I want land where I can build sustainable, beautiful, sacred spaces. I want to create as much financial success as possible so that I can use it for increasing awareness and change in our less-than-preferable situations. I'd like to be able to contribute to businesses and non-profits that need support and are already "doing the work".

Here's a thought for today: How can things change if there's nothing to be changed? If we want forward momentum, we need the "thing" to depart from into the next "thing". Seeing what we "don't want" allows us to refocus and clearly define what we "do want". As much as I prefer not to see addicts strewn across the Ventura Pier, I know there is a new earth waiting to be realized. I know that through my consciousness and that of others, we can and will create changes. It starts with our own energy and intention. If I allow what I see to determine how I vibrate today, it will be a very depressing day. But if I use the "sludge" to create the conscious decision to be as empowered as possible, the negative I see will begin to lessen in comparison to the beauty I will see.

Today I will write and share my passion. Today I will read mind and heart-stimulating material. Today I will attend Lokpal's healing/meditation session (a dear local spiritual teacher). Today I will talk to people I love who speak with positive words and have a trust in the beauty that is just around the corner. Actually, it's already here. It's you, and me, and the ones awakening every second across the globe. Isn't that exciting? Like I said, the winds are-a-changin' and thank Goddess!

Book of the day – *The Road to Shambhala* by Gerald Stanek
Quote of the day – "When we follow the spirit, countless worlds are constantly opening before us, and in those worlds there are pastures green everywhere." – From *The Pathway of Roses* by Christian Larson

HAPPINESS FACTORS

Day 41 – September 23, 2014 – 11:03 a.m.

I've taken inventory of many of the people in my life, those I know well as well as others I know on a lesser basis, and even the people I see around social media on a consistent basis.

I asked myself, "Are there any people who *feel* authentically happy to me?" (At bare minimum, more often than not.) The things people talk about are not always an indication of whether they are happy. For example, talking about your children, home, and vacation doesn't make you happy. It's how people *feel* to me, vibrationally, when they speak or when I am in their field. I make this distinction because we often get stuck in external trappings of what happiness is. "I have two kids. My husband has a great job. We're vacationing in Bali next week." But I'm touching more on the inner knowingness we have when we're around happy people.

There are a few people I can think of who feel authentically happy, on a regular basis to me. This doesn't mean they don't have a challenge come up or feel emotions when someone passes away, etc. It just means they generally have a positive outlook, convey deep feelings of joy, and when I am around them, my light gets even brighter. They also convey great amounts of gratitude and a few other qualities I will mention below. The main point is that when you bathe in their energy, you feel it. It's a knowingness that a happy person is right there in front of you. It's infectious, in fact.

Why is it that the self-proclaimed "happy" people I know are in years of therapy sessions, on pharmaceuticals, or worse? Where is the void? Why are the people with nice homes, nice cars, and nice family units perpetually stressed out, ranting or complaining, aggressively weaving through traffic, and rarely conveying pure joy? The level of anxiety, panic attacks, negativity, depression, and feeling of being lost is rampant in my communities both online and off.

I can think of one couple I know who work from home, have two online businesses, virtually perfect health, and are always beaming from ear to ear in what I can tell are definitely not fake smiles. I took a closer look (observed for several years) and realized that they have the *exact* same qualities as other happy people I know in my personal life. These are:
- They take absolutely no pharmaceutical medications.
- They spend countless hours in nature every day.
- They grow much of their own food, source some locally, and eat a vegetarian, organic diet. (I also know happy people who are meat eaters. This is not a food lecture.)
- They have total financial freedom, work from their homes, and only produce products and services they are wildly passionate about. While they are *able* to buy anything, they only buy what

they need and what speaks to them. Money is not an obsession, despite how blessed they are.

- They are in perfect health (from what I can see of their transparent health posts online).
- They speak with words that are carefully chosen to incite only positive outcomes.
- They do not, under any circumstance, complain or give promotion to any negativity happening in the world.
- They are teachable, always reading and educating themselves on many levels.
- They have a network of people, both locally and online that they interact with and share their teachings.
- They are in a loving, committed, healthy relationship.
- They are extremely active, whether doing martial arts, yoga, or taking long walks.
- They do not allow the weather to dictate whether they will go outside.
- They are spontaneous and adventurous.
- They live simply, with no extravagant unnecessary "stuff" lying around, but rather carefully chosen placement of things that have meaning.
- They each have separate dreams and passions as well as some that overlap. They support one another fully.
- They each meditate every day and spend quiet time alone, writing and working.
- They are conscious of the environment.
- They give service of their time and also value their time, charging appropriately for it.

That's the tip of the iceberg, but it affirms what I wish to help people with... to discover and expand into a spiritual journey (living your happiest and best life possible) through a connection to nature, people (including yourself), and a life of purpose. All of the "happy" people I know have all three of these, relatively consistently in their lives. They need not always be perfectly balanced, but they touch on all three consistently throughout their lifetimes. Happiness seems to be naturally birthed by people who harmonize these three qualities.

My brother, Kobe. He is a great smiler!

There is no pill, therapy session, coach, or anything else outside yourself that will bring happiness. It truly starts from within. We can begin slowly shifting our choices, our surroundings, our words, our outlook, our activities, and our self-worth. These shifts will work themselves into a beautiful cycle of joy created upon joy created upon joy....

I can't say I am happy 100% of the time, but I am certainly coming close and I have learned how to bring myself back to my natural happy birthright when I find myself sinking. And isn't that the mission - to know how to find your way back when you get lost? It's not about being perfect. It's about creating more and more opportunities of goodness in your life from which happiness is naturally birthed. And how blessed we are to feel these beautiful things in the first place!

While there's no exact recipe, many of the happiness factors listed above may be calling to you. If so, see how you might incorporate one or two of them starting...now!

Current Book (a must read) – *The Road to Shambhala* by my friend Gerald Stanek.

Quote of the Day – "Man sacrifices his health to make money. Then he sacrifices money to recuperate his health. And then he is so anxious about the future that he does not enjoy the present; the result being that he does not live in the present or the future. He lives as if he is never going to die, and then dies having never really lived." – Dalai Lama

COMMERCIAL ZOMBIELAND

Day 43 – September 25, 2014 – 1:30 p.m.

Have you ever watched anything on internet television? I attempted to watch something today on a network and when I was about midway through a movie, a new type of commercial popped up. A screen appeared offering me a few options.

1. Click here for an interactive commercial.
2. Click here for a general commercial instead.
3. If you do not click one of the two options, we will play an even longer commercial than the other two.

The media often fogs our minds until we can't see what's clearly right in front of us.

Essentially, the computer commercial was threatening me with longer commercials if I did not play its game. This is a huge piece of evidence in the case file I call *Commercial Zombie Land: Controlling the Masses*. We are slowly becoming unconscious, screen-addicted robots and we do whatever a lifeless piece of machinery with no emotions tells us to do. Really think about that and let it settle in. If you are able, let it settle in so you can *feel* that. How does it feel to be given two options and if you don't pick, you're screwed?

Here's a human example of what just happened online:

1. Do you want the peanut butter and fish guts sandwich you hate? (Annoying commercial A)
2. Or do you want just the fish guts sandwich by itself? (Annoying commercial B)
3. If you don't pick one of those two, you will be forced to eat a sandwich you hate even more. This will be peanut butter, fish guts, and rotten eggs. (Annoying and Ungodly lengthy commercial C)

This blog is simply a call to be very conscious when you are using technology or viewing the media. Do you really want to let certain things into your psyche? Do you accept that a computer will be dictating commands, knowing most people will obey while very few will watch the longer commercial (Or even better, log off entirely and take back the power!)? If you don't want to be a zombie, don't visit Zombie Land.

I find myself spending less and less time watching shows or participating in any of this; and therefore I stay sharp and aware of the programming that goes on. I spot it and refuse to play.

Follow your truth out of the fog and into the light.

Do you participate at the gas pump when the television screen begins playing? Do you think it's fair to have something distracting you in hopes you will spend more money at the pump? I look away. I will not watch the gas station television. Period. Demand your local gas station remove their zombie televisions.

I don't often focus on what's "wrong" in the world. But every once in a while I have a heightened sensation about something and this was definitely something worth tapping into. Only, of course, to create good out of the realization that something negative is taking place. Today was a wake-up call, a realization of being threatened by a commercial. The masses do not notice. They are unconscious. Or if they do notice, it's mildly annoying and they just want to get to the movie they're watching. They figure it can't hurt to listen to the commands. But each time we are accepting these commands into our consciousness, we are telling the world, "Please command me to do what you want. Please put my brain on passive mode. Please do not allow me the freedom to make my own choices."

Alternative zombies unite! There's a wild, free, creative, beautiful world moving itself into being this very moment. We are creating it through being conscious of what we will and will not allow. Some of you may have jived with these ideas years ago. You get it. For those of you who are having some cognitions, congratulate yourself! It's a new day. Go forth and be free, my friends! You have expanded your DNA and I am very excited for you!

Thank you for taking a journey into Commercial Zombie Land with me. I'll see you soon in Consciousness Land! (We must first acknowledge what is happening, turn our backs on it, and re-focus on what we *do* want!)

At first, you may be the only one on the bench. But in time, others will join you.

Current Book – Still reading *The Road to Shambhala* by Gerald Stanek.
Quote of the Day – "Don't ever think I fell for you, or fell over you. I didn't fall in love, I rose in it."- Toni Morrison

MY INNER BOBCAT

Day 44 – September 26, 2014 – 6:35 p.m.

There are so many internal shifts happening every day. It's as if I am living several months of learning in one day. It's hard to explain, but it feels as if time is speeding up, such that within a twenty four hour period, I've moved through the experiences, emotions, and learning of several months. This is all part of the awakening, or the shift in consciousness, and is being felt all over the world. When we embark on a spiritual journey, or set the intention to drop into a spiritual experience, the universe hears and perhaps delivers a super-speed roller-coaster experience of growth.

Yesterday was beautiful and emotional. I joined my online mastermind team, who I've been meeting with weekly for several months. It's been transformative on many levels, predominantly in forming relationships of depth with several of them. I missed last week's session due to my grandfather passing away and in the interim, made a decision to step away for a month or more to focus on income and my website. My finances do not currently allow me to continue with the group. I am not paying for the mastermind we all contribute to nor the coaching sessions I was getting (I was gifted with some free ones when my major financial troubles hit.). It was fine for a while, but suddenly it did not feel like a fair exchange. What felt authentic to me was to focus on income and to pay my way when I am able (if my internal guidance system directs me back). Most people would also call me "crazy" for stopping coaching sessions with a wonderful person, a caring heart, someone who has made a lot of money, and could potentially teach me to do the same. However, it's not always the surface that shows the reality. The truth is, somewhere deep down inside a knowingness called out that said:

1. There's nothing I can't do through my personal power.
2. My coach was sidetracked developing his program and it would actually be a gift to him to free up his time and then re-group when he has more time to focus on coaching.
3. Ongoing free coaching is really not an exchange at abundance (meaning each person is getting greater value that what they are putting in, or initially expected) or an even exchange (meaning each person is putting equal value of something they are exchanging such as money for service).
4. I feel unchallenged and un-stimulated, like I'm wading through syrup during the sessions instead of launching myself forward effectively. I've told several friends that the type of mentor I have must be able to keep up with me. My mind is sharp, my intuition is keen, and I rarely find someone who challenges me and carries me forward effectively. That's not about thinking I'm better than anyone else. I simply have a need for a strong mentor and I've not yet found someone who can both keep up with me and also completely respect my sense of integrity. Rather I find mentors that seem to resonate for a while and then I reach a knowingness to let them go.

While others might think I am a complete nut-job, I feel so empowered with making this choice. I feel a sense of integrity, and a sense of spiritual alignment. The true authentic Julie, the soul within, creates abundant exchanges and also speaks her truth when receiving clear guidance about something. We are taught to fear coaches, mentors, leaders, judges, and teachers. But the real ones will listen, take responsibility where needed, and hand you responsibility where you need it. And it was a wonderful reinforcement of my own lesson I teach others - to speak your truth even when it doesn't make sense to the mind of yourself or others. If your soul/gut speaks it, let your voice speak it. It's important for me to live this when I ask others to live this so often - it keeps me congruent.

I broke down in the mastermind, crying as I shared that I had no money to contribute and would have to leave for a month or more. I explained that I am living out of my truck, but also on a very powerful adventure and feeling more happy and blessed than ever. The responses were so beautiful, both the appreciation of my emotional release and also a reflection of my ability to articulate, my power as a woman, and the confidence in my offerings to the world, so that felt very wonderful. Sometimes we don't take the time to let compliments or positive feedback really sink in. I did that and allowed myself to really feel it.

Yesterday was a journey of truly feeling without thinking or worrying. I felt the knowingness to break away for a while, from a spiritual place deep in my soul. And I felt the love reflected to me by my friends. It was truly a beautiful day.

Last night I dreamed of a bobcat. I think it was trying to drink water and I remember attempting or wondering if I should interact with it, as it was so powerful. I believe I did end up coming in contact with the cat and feeling its power. The dream started to fade. Bobcats are symbolic of patience; they are solitary creatures and therefore symbolize the need to step back from those around us (like I did yesterday), and unleash our inner hidden secrets and talents. Certainly makes sense considering the type of day I had!

What would your inner bobcat allow you to unleash?

Current Book – *On the Road* by Jack Kerouac
Quote of the Day – "Boys and girls in America have such a sad time together; sophistication demands that they submit to sex immediately, without proper preliminary talk. Not courting talk — real straight talk about souls, for life is holy and every moment is precious."- By Jack Kerouac

MAGICAL HEALING SESSIONS

Day 44 – September 26, 2014 – 7:07 p.m.

I'll likely touch on several magical experiences at Lokpal's house. I use the term "magic" loosely. Please don't mistake "magic" with something fluffy, fake, or a "trick" performed by a magician. My personal use of the word "magic" signifies the happenings beyond mind understanding. The tendency is to rely on the mind to explain away, through logic, certain things that can't possibly happen in the "normal" world. (Actually, they can and do happen, but this is based on society's assumed expectations of what's "normal".) What I've learned about my own magical experiences is that they take place through my own openness and creation, and are more felt than understood. They're like E.T.'s trail of Reese's Pieces leading the way. My magic and miracles are a trail of signs, helping me move through the world with a knowingness that all is well and I am on path.

A great peace exists and is accessible anytime you choose it.

Lokpal is a spiritual healer/teacher here in Ojai. People show up by word of mouth; ya don't find this guy on Google. This is kind of appealing and refreshing and also curious, as he could have a lot more traffic with a site. However, I trust he is in touch with spirit, following his own guidance to do what's best for him. Perhaps his guides have asked that he not get world exposure and to keep things modest. Sometimes less is more. I find I still get trapped in the expectation that "success" means exposure to the world and I've learned there are many definitions of success. Following your own guidance and bliss is most important, of course. In any case, Friday healing afternoons with Lokpal have been life-transforming on so many levels. I have an amazing story about manifesting crystals that I will likely save for another time. In the meantime, I'll share some of the magical moments I've had at Lokpal's and perhaps they will inspire new thoughts and feelings along your own spiritual journey.

Today I walked into the room where Lokpal's attendees gather. I sat in a reserved seat up front because I have been giving service by smudging everyone before he comes out to do the healing. We typically begin by watching conscious videos and then he does energy healing as he walks around the room. There are many entities present that work through him. Lokpal is a conscious medium, so he is fully awake and aware through everything; they just use his instrument (body) to focus the healing. We later reflect on the healing and meditation, sharing experiences and also talking about the videos or asking questions of those he channels. It is a deeply spiritual, fun, relaxed, sacred environment. The people are wonderful and soft in spirit. I cherish these few hours every week with Lokpal very much.

I went to sit on my chair today and saw some jasmine sandalwood essential oil on it. What a special way to walk into a session. I later learned this was a gift for my sage service each week, but I feel I receive a gift just by being of service. This is an example of Lokpal's giving heart. When he found out I had moved into my truck he bought me some shower gel and a fluffy towel and left them for me at a session. I'm so filled with the energetic gifts I get there; the physical gifts were like an overflow of extra goodness.

Smudging people is a wonderful experience. Not only does the smell of the sage put me in tune with Mother Earth, my heart, and clear the air; it also makes me feel very connected with the people in the room. I find myself having more psychic or clairsentient experiences as I sage people. Today a teenager who sometimes attends said he was having some fluttering sensations in his upper chest. I could feel that as I smudged him and had the sensation of wanting to put my hand right on his chest. I refrained so I wouldn't freak him out as he entered into meditation. He's probably about nineteen years old or so and totally tuned in to the "truth" despite his parents wanting things for him that go against his inner knowledge. I am really proud of him for listening to his inner drum and following himself into this spiritual journey. Anyway, these types of experiences happen more and more at Lokpal's sessions.

Open up. Allow yourself to receive!

I also feel entities working on me. Today I felt someone lean down around my knee and blow air on it once, like some type of breath work for healing. It felt similar to some Huna healing I experienced several years ago. When we came out of meditation, I asked Lokpal why he was blowing on my knee (which was inflamed) and he started laughing. He was nowhere near my knee. This is just the tip of the iceberg regarding my healing sessions. I began attending regularly around six months ago when I went through a very painful breakup. I believe it's one of the reasons why I survived much of what I have been through. The non-religious, but fully welcoming and loving environment connects me to spirit every time. Fridays are the days I currently live for. These sessions provide oxygen to my soul. I see so much craziness on the road, and so many people are feeling the chaos during "the shift". Coming here regularly and having a true spiritual practice is really a blessing.

One "a-ha" I've had by attending Lokpal's sessions is we have to choose it for ourselves. A spiritual practice doesn't just "happen" automatically. Most people won't go. They will be tired, or busy, or find a reason not to attend. But when you commit to a spiritual practice, the return is exponential. It takes a commitment to yourself and the willingness to follow through on that commitment. Walking out of Lokpal's sessions each week felt so incredible; it was easy to keep that commitment to myself. And I'm so glad I did!

More from magical Lokpal's house soon. I send him a big overflowing thank you and hugs from my heart!

Current Book – *On The Road* by Jack Kerouac
Quote of the Day – "...the only people for me are the mad ones, the ones who are mad to live, mad to talk, mad to be saved, desirous of everything at the same time, the ones who never yawn or say a commonplace thing, but burn, burn, burn like fabulous yellow roman

candles exploding like spiders across the stars." – Jack Kerouac from the book above

I'M STILL JUDGEMENTAL (SOMETIMES)

Day 45 – September 27, 2014 – 9:19 p.m.

My friends invited me to comedy night in the Ventura Harbor tonight. We've been there many times, usually for gay comedy night. This time we thought we'd venture out into the big wide world of straight people. Ha! Just kidding. Gotta' joke with ourselves sometimes. The fact that we even separate the two is hilarious.

One of the comedians was super raunchy, risqué, obnoxious – really "out there". His comedy was nothing worse than we would see on television, but enough to get some resistance from the crowd and some uncertain, hesitant laughs. I was watching my thought process, noticing I was making certain judgments about what this person must be like off stage (which is entirely irrelevant). Without giving words to it in my head, I noticed that I assumed he was a jerk or an old washed up, bitter comedian who drank too much (his act included spilling beer on himself).

At the end of his act, he said a special comedian wanted to come to the stage. It was his teenage daughter who had down syndrome and she told a knock-knock joke. It was very sweet and endearing. He was sensitive and wonderful with her. My whole body released, realizing I had been making unfair assessments and confusing an act with reality. How often do we assume an actor is just like his character? How often do we meet someone who is perhaps nervous or stressed and assume they are nuts in every aspect of their lives? I put myself in check today, noticing my own judgments that were unfair. I don't know that comedian from beans. To assume who he is in real life is irrelevant and impossible - and also none of my business unless I will be interacting with him on a personal level. I simply hired him to be funny, and while not my favorite comedian, he was still pretty dang talented.

101

I made a choice to honor him in my mind, and to forgive myself for a less-than-spiritual assessment. Spiritual journeys truly bring us to a variety of places, including the realization of our downfalls, judgments, and areas we need growth. I pretty darn near love everyone, for the pure reverence of their humanity. But I slip out of that sometimes, and get better and better at placing myself right back on the escalator to unconditional love. This is one of the most important things I feel a spiritual journey can bring me – to a place of pure love, where unnecessary judgments are no longer capable of rearing their heads. I'm not talking about general deductions and judgments we must intuit every day such as, "This parking lot feels safer than that one. I will park here under the lights."

I'm talking about judging other people without enough facts, or pigeonholing people when it's not appropriate. What a relief to let go after I realized what I had done. And interestingly, as soon as I let go of the judgment I had toward the comedian, he looked different to me. He looked softer, or slightly more handsome. Fascinating, indeed. Our vibration, our light, affects every single thing – even the way we perceive others.

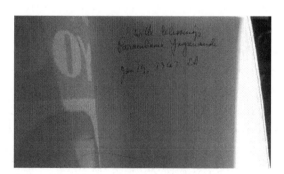

Another wonderful surprise came today. A while back I purchased a copy of *Autobiography of a Yogi* at Goodwill for fifty cents or so. Inside the cover, on the right hand side, Paramahansa Yogananda signed his name and wrote "With blessings" and the date of January 19, 1947, the year after it was released. For the next several months I was under the impression the signature was a real one done in pen rather than a photocopy printed with the book. My blood was pumping with excitement and I felt as if this great sage was sitting by my side, enveloping me with love.

Several months later I looked more closely at the black ink. It was, indeed, a photocopy of his original signature. He must have wanted all of his books to contain his blessing and signature. At first I was bummed out. Then I stepped back, realizing I made an incorrect assessment of a material object. Whether that signature was "real" or not, I received a great blessing and deep feelings of connection to this yogi. What matters more than that? Nothing! I'm not interested in selling a signed book for money. I'm not interested in showing off the book. I simply felt excited over the connection I felt, which happened regardless of the "realness" of that signature.

My choice was not to judge the situation as a let-down, but to continue to awaken and feel the connection we can tap into of great teachers who blessed us with so much love and grace (even the teachers who appear as raunchy comedians)!

Current Book – *On the Road* by Jack Kerouac
Quote of the Day – "Success is not rightly measured by the worldly standards of wealth, prestige and power. None of these bestow happiness unless they are rightly used. To use them rightly one must possess wisdom and love for God and man."- Paramahansa Yogananda

THOSE DANG POP-UP WINDOWS

Day 50 – October 2, 2014

I downloaded someone's eBook today and had to type in my email address. That's fine; it's obvious the intention behind giving away free product is the company then gets access to you on behalf of selling more things. Nothing would ever get sold if everyone gave away everything for free, so I find it's a fair trade to contact me in exchange for some free information I desire. I'm now like a pre-qualified customer that may be interested in other offerings or information down the line.

However, there is one thing happening frequently throughout websites and social media that is a huge turnoff. When I am reading instructions to download information, browsing things to purchase, or reading a blog – suddenly a screen pops up blocking my view of what I'm engaged in. It's like a not-so-subtle way of saying, "Hey! I don't care that you were engaged in something. I am desperate for you to see this right now and buy more stuff because I am afraid you won't see it unless I interrupt you!"

I call this "internet face".

Of course it would be unfair and judgmental to assume every business owner who chooses to create these pop-ups has poor intentions. But the use of these pop-up boxes makes several assumptions that might ultimately do the opposite of what they're created to do (drive sales). Here are a few of the assumptions these pop-up creators make:

Assumption #1 – It's okay to interrupt people.
Why is it acceptable to interrupt someone on a computer if it wouldn't be acceptable at the dinner table? For example, your friend asks you what your favorite piece of art is at the local gallery. You begin sharing some ideas with her and mid-sentence she says, "Guess what?! I knew you were an art fiend so I wanted to see if you'd like to take the art class around the corner starting next week." The question about the art gallery was just bait. She wasn't actually interested in your answer. She just needed a way to get you into the art class. This is how pop-up windows work. A company sends someone to a page they will engage with. Then the company allows itself to interrupt the viewer's activity on behalf

of its own agenda. In my opinion, it's the responsibility of the company to make their offerings obvious without the need to interrupt me every few seconds as I am attempting to review the first offering.

Assumption #2 – Your clients won't mind being interrupted.
While there may be some robots out there that don't care, I find it highly disruptive. Every time a pop-up box rears its head, I must spend time clicking off options to return to what I was doing. Often I leave the sites permanently to avoid any more of this annoyance.

Assumption #3 – Desperation and impatience win the game.
These two qualities almost always turn me away from a salesperson or a website. If I'm engaged on your site, I'm an engaged customer. Do you want a disengaged customer? The fastest way to do that is to break someone's concentration, distract them, and make them feel you desperately need something from them. Sometimes the snail wins the race. There's nothing wrong with allowing someone to read your blog without interruption. You've spent hours writing, editing, photographing, and much more. Why do you want to interrupt the experience of enjoying your gift you've given on behalf of "sealing the deal" right away? If someone spends twenty minutes on my website and doesn't buy anything but loves the information and trusts me, that's worth all the "sales" in the world. That person may stick with me for years, eventually buying things through trust versus impulse. Do I want everyone to sign up for my newsletter the second they start engaging on my site? Not really. I want everyone who *really wants* what I have to offer to sign up for my newsletter. It's about the quality of the customer, not the quantity. Maybe the companies who constantly interrupt people will get a few more sign-ups beyond me. But most of those people will likely unsubscribe, versus the customer who is actively engaged and seeks out more of your information.

Assumption #4 – Your potential customers/clients are not intelligent.

There exists an understanding that we must hold our potential customer's hand or else they are entirely clueless. Imagine that someone has come to your website and is reading, downloading, looking, inquiring, etc. They are obviously doing something important, or you would not have any of those pages they are enjoying. The pages guide the customer where to go next. Assuming they need a giant flashing screen that pops up out of nowhere is assuming they are not intelligent enough to find what they need. The most common pop-up screens include, "Sign up for my newsletter" and "Check out our great specials this week!" Is the customer so dumb, they do not know how to click on the "products" tab and scroll down to the "specials" link? Can the customer not clearly see the newsletter sign up box to the right of the blog they are reading? I can't speak for anyone else, but when I am deeply engaged in a blog, a product I'm looking at, or some other information on a website, I have to be virtually torn away from the site. I'm stuck like glue to whatever task is at hand. Rarely do I leave a site because I can't find the "products" tab or the "newsletter" sign up. I do, however, leave when screens constantly pop up at me, annoying me, and making me want to bash the computer in. People are smart. They can find what they need. Let them find it.

The tech world and spiritual world can unite forces!

This is a strange topic for a spiritually-based blog/book I'm creating. We tend to think the spiritual world and computer world are separate. But they are reflections (or can be) of one another. I want to have the same degree of spiritual integrity with my website and sales tactics as I do in my "real" life. I don't want to interrupt you right now. You might be having a great realization. Or you might be sending this blog to someone. Perhaps you'll forget to share it if I interrupt you to make you go to my Amazon store and buy a bunch of things. You should have the respect and right to click where you want on this site without being yelled at by windows I create. I'm glad you're here. I'm blessed that you are here engaging with ideas that are near and dear to my heart. You, having trust in me, is my first and foremost mission here. There are no *quality* sales built from a vibration of annoyance, distrust, desperation, etc. I believe there is a truly ethical way to disseminate technology. We forget our manners, assuming "real life" grace is not needed on media platforms. In truth, we need much more care and consideration for how we treat people within the technology world.

I hope you enjoyed reading this blog today pop-up free!

Current book - *On The Road* by Jack Kerouac
Quote of the Day - "I just won't sleep," I decided. There were so many other interesting things to do. – Jack Kerouac from the book above

THE HEART OF MAY AND DINNER FOR TONY BENNETT?!

Day 51 – October 3, 2014 – 8:06 p.m.

I left my friend May's house after spending three nights camping on her land, high above Santa Barbara. She lives near the Chumash painted caves, a very sacred and spiritual Native American space.

Paintings in the Chumash cave

Yesterday I helped May for a short while in the kitchen. She's a local caterer focusing on fresh organic food. No matter what, I always taste something divine when we hang out. May lives an extraordinary life. One would never know this as she's one of the most down to earth and understated people I know. Her wit is quick. She's perennially open to learning and growing. May tends to deflect compliments and not acknowledge what a giving heart she has. Thank Goddess a few of us out there recognize it and share it with her; she deserves it!

Here are just a few of the things she's done for me during my temporary financial challenges:

- Bought a ticket to an event that was about $600 and trusted me to pay her back when the money arrived. I did.

- Paid for a hotel room when we attended an event through a private organization we belonged to. There was no need to pay her back. I was later able to gift her with a room I had one time, but it wasn't out of "owing her". It just happened nicely and I was so glad to share in return.
- The other night we went to a live local concert. We were hungry and May automatically paid after choosing a nice Italian restaurant. I didn't expect her to pay. In fact, I tried not to let her because I didn't want to be the "burden" that shows up on her land and then expects dinner, but she insisted. May has a massive amount of grace and class about these things. She understands without being condescending or ever making me feel like I'm unsuccessful or unworthy.
- She sent me off with a sandwich, some cheese, and a watermelon she couldn't use after helping her with some catering stuff.

Such is the heart of May. Goodness seems to be effortless for her and my hopes are that she might recognize what a wonderful quality this is when she reads this. She's tender in special moments and has shed a tear with me here and there. But May is also slightly guarded and sometimes I wonder if she takes in the love available to her.

Back to the catering - In addition to being an extraordinary person, May lives an amazing life. By shear will of her mind and heart, she went from a newbie caterer of parties of about twenty-five to catering Jackson Browne's fundraiser of three-hundred-fifty people. Talk about synchronicity, manifestation, and a spiritual journey! May creates things that the Average Joe would consider quite remarkable.

After I helped May move some kitchen freezer boxes around and did some dishes, I helped her gather a few food items for someone she kept referring to as "Tony". She would say, "Tony is going to love this, I hope!" Or, "Should I put all of the crackers on Tony's plate or just the plain ones?"

I felt some very powerful energy at the Chumash cave. And my time with May was about feeling loved. Here is a photo I took just outside the cave as I left May's land. Notice the heart of light!

The gourmet food goodies were set in the car and suddenly I realized we were dropping the food off for the one and only Tony Bennett! I put it all together after May said we needed to park at the Granada Theater where Tony is performing tonight. I said, "May! You're making food for Tony BENNETT?!"

"Yeah, why?"

I exclaimed, "For the last couple hours I had no idea 'Tony' was *The Tony.*"

We sort of giggled and then dropped off the food to Tony's assistants. Tony was likely busy rehearsing or relaxing, so we didn't get to see this amazing icon. (There was a beautiful androgynous gal on security duty, which also made the visit worth it. But let me not digress!)

Tony Bennett is eighty-eight years young. And May gets to cater for him. She's also deeply close with Joe Cocker. And she's a helicopter pilot. That's just the tip of the iceberg. It's not that being friends with famous people validates us. It's just an example of some of the remarkable aspects of May that one would never know unless you got to know her.

Here's my point: Connection is so important. It's one of my three main principles of my business – nature, connection, and purpose. May is one of the many connections I have who fill my experience with goodness. And she has connections that fill her with goodness.

Sunset in Santa Barbara while we walked May's pup.

Who are you connected to? Who do you feel close with? Do you have extraordinary friends? Do you have people you love and respect and who trust you, support you, respect you and teach you about yourself? If not, now's the time to create connections. It will profoundly change your life for the better!

Current Book – *Clear Body Clear Mind* by L. Ron Hubbard (I find most people have fear or assumptions surrounding certain books such as this one. When I sense fear, I delve in and find answers for myself. This book actually has some interesting information in it. Often we don't hear about many "facts"; we always hear about the sensationalized crud. For example, the purification program listed in this book was gifted to many people who suffered from smoke inhalation/chemical exposure after the 9/11 event in New York. Isn't it interesting how the media twists things, yet you never hear about some of the good things that came from Hubbard? Sometimes reading is not about discovering if someone or something is good or bad, but to discover if something feels vibrationally aligned for you, personally. There's an art to listening to your own guidance. Begin with releasing fear, listening, and researching to discover your own answers!)

Quote of the Day – "When reading a book, be very certain that you never go past a word you do not fully understand. The only reason a person gives up a study or becomes confused or unable to learn is because he or she has gone past a word that was not understood." – L. Ron Hubbard

SALAD DRESSING FROM 1912

Day 53 – October 5, 2014 – 10:26 a.m.

I'm watching an adorable little dachshund at a beautiful Ojai home. It feels great to have a home to myself for the week. After a while, I feel a little disheveled and my car looks like a tornado hit it. There's a fine art to keeping a car organized when most of what you need is in it. I do have a storage unit (small one) for most of my belongings, but many items travel with me.

House sitting always provides interesting people and experiences. I've discovered in addition to attracting all sorts of typical "spiritual" things like new sacred sites, labyrinths, etc., part of what I am attracting are people and situations that provide the opportunity to really walk the talk. The home I am currently in is a massive, beautiful place but a depressive energy resides here. Cheese from 2010 is living (apparently permanently) in the refrigerator. Almost every condiment bottle is rancid. I found ranch dressing from 2009 (for my future readers, the date of this entry is 2014)! The homeowners keep an inventory sheet listing masses of food and extra freezers for God only knows what. I am all for storing up in case of an emergency, but when you waste this much stuff on a consistent basis, I think it would be wiser to clear out and keep less until one learns the art of using what you have before you get more. I was offered any and all of the food I want while I stay, but I dare touch nothing! My breakfast was a bag of free oranges from my friend Randee.

Fresh Ojai oranges. Delicious!

There are also buckets of medications and vitamins here. Around every corner are major depression, anxiety, and emotional disorder medications. They are not neatly tucked away, but rather spread out openly on the counter. As I opened bathroom cabinets to find a replacement roll of toilet paper, I saw more and more of the same and other medications (enough to carry a person through a whole lifetime). *All* of the people here are heavily medicated. They all have neuroses and/or depressions of some kind. The dog has also adopted this, as she has some nervous habits. Hoards of records, books, lotions, potions, and even spices from ten years ago cover most surfaces. Nearly everything here is rotten or something I would fear eating if it was served to me. Yet there are juxtapositions such as beautiful art and craftwork, nice leather furniture, and areas of care and attention.

When I arrived to meet the homeowners (this was a referred job), they reeked of misery. One of them could barely look me in the eye. The other was in bed in the middle of the afternoon watching television in the dark. Another had breath that smelled like the foulest rot I could ever imagine. I don't share these details to belittle people. I share because when I enter someone's space; I must choose to drop down into my heart center or sink into despair.

Backyard Ojai view over the orchards. One of the many blessings of house sitting!

This family needs a lot of compassion (as well as deep emotional help). There is little to no chance anything will ever change in their lives. I can just feel it. But what can I do while I am here?

I began by choosing to be my happy self when I met them. I smiled, was warm and friendly, and did not act like I was judging any of the toxic food or medications they were loading up for their week away. I sent them as much healing light as possible when I thought about how unhappy they must be (and prayed they would not get in an accident from being over-medicated). I also created the intention to bring my own light and happiness to this home while I am here – perhaps they will feel it when they arrive.

I am also being very conscious about my own emotional state in this space. It would be easy to slide into depression, as the air is thick with apathy, the rooms are dark, and there is clutter around every corner. I remain in a state of gratitude for the opportunity to enjoy this beautiful home, to cuddle this sweet pup I am watching (who cuddles me *every* moment of the day and night), and to perhaps bring just a minute or two of smiles into the family's life before I head out.

Staying in someone's home is a tender experience, especially when I'm just a "house sitter" versus family. People trust me to be in their space, and I take that very close to my heart. I appreciate that people can sense my energy, knowing I respect their spaces and take the most ridiculously over-attentive care of their animals ever! Because I've done masses of sitting over the years, I've experienced very toxic depressive homes like this one and also very open, organized, bright, cheery places. I run with crowds of very conscious, earth-friendly, happy people and this place is not the usual in a long list of places I've stayed.

It's very interesting, in a certain way, to get to know people based on their belongings/spaces. As it turns out, the happiest people I know are the ones who have little to no clutter, no piles of expired food, no piles of junk, and use the least toxic substances. Connection? I think so! More on that stuff in the future; back to the topic at hand!

It's my *choice* to be a spiritual person living in this human body. I can *choose* to compassionately see the pain in this family, wish them well, and move forward. Hopefully by reading this entry, just one family will recognize a part of themselves, have a small awakening, and make some shifts, not out of judgment, but purely by looking at the facts. We fear facts. They're just facts. That's what makes them so beautiful! We don't have to wrap emotion into them. For example, "This is my pile of newspapers that need to be moved to the recycle bin. This is my dirty dish that belongs in the kitchen. That piece of laundry can go in the laundry basket instead of on the floor."

When we get emotional about these facts and start thinking, "I'm a slob. I'm worthless. I can't even wash my friggin' plate," we tend to continue the downward spiral. We need to start asking ourselves factually based questions to begin the process of clearing out spaces (which then clears the mind).
"Is my space neat and clean? Do I hold on to things that are not usable? Am I on medications that I don't truly need to be on? Do I take care of personal hygiene necessities such as brushing my teeth and washing my socks?"

Some of us find it truly unbelievable that people never ask themselves these basic questions. Or if they do, they ignore the answers that come up. I have absolutely no shyness about saying that I've had piles of papers and "to-do" boxes throughout my house. But I have a dialogue with myself about them and do something about these areas. I get better each year, but I'm not perfect. Living in my car helps. It forces me to decide what I actually need day to day. Sometimes I store too much. Other times I wish I had more. It's a process of finding a balance, which is ultimately what I think this whole blog is about. As I began to write, I didn't really know what it was about. I just knew I had to start writing about this wild place with the salad dressing from 1912 (wink wink), and here we are!

The external and internal reflect each other. They show us our areas of imbalance and balance. If you have scones in your pantry from last year, this may be a good time to focus on balancing your spaces and belongings. Asking yourself what might need balancing internally is also a powerful thing to do. Some people begin working with the mind and emotions. As they increase experiences of love and happiness, the external reflects it. Suddenly spaces clear and flowers grace the counter. Other people need to clear spaces and bring flowers in to help the mind feel a sense of peace and balance. Whichever is your method, allow it to help you through the moments of overwhelm.

And remember to never stop loving yourself immensely, piles or none.

Current book – *The Way to Happiness* by L. Ron Hubbard (While I disagree with several premises in this book, some aspects of it are worth tapping into. As mentioned in my last blog, it's healthy to read things we've been taught are "wrong" without originally having made that decision ourselves. Reading things we both agree and disagree with is an excellent tool to exercise and sharpen our intuition. I highly recommend you read a book you've been told will scar you for life. Often it's funny how powerless these "scary" things are when we begin to judge for ourselves!)
Quote of the day – "Try to be a rainbow in someone's cloud." – Maya Angelou

HOOKING UP TO A SPIRITUAL I.V.

Day 64 – October 16, 2014 – 8:00 a.m.

Just over two months ago I left my home. Time has flown by fairly quickly. I believe I've spent less than fourteen days of that in my car, so I know for sure I'm having a very different home(less) experience than those I see sleeping on cardboard or bundled in blankets on benches.

This week has been full of both spiritual and healing experiences, as well as concentrated time with friends. This week I checked "Meditate with a Buddhist Monk" off my bucket list. I was gathered at a meeting with other friends from a personal development club I'm involved with. We tend to explore all sorts of empowered activities together and our meetings include helping each other overcome challenges using a round table mastermind system of sorts. The time we spend in each meeting is *always* full of "aha" moments we call "cognitions", deep friendships, and lots of love.

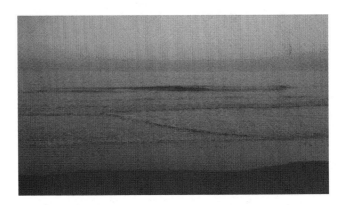

I also experienced my first few *Dianetics* auditing sessions this week. While I was always trained by the fear-inducing media to stay clear of this at all costs and that Scientology is on par with the Devil, I talked with a friend who was having tangible results using the auditing

119

process. Neither one of us is interested in being Scientologists, joining the church (or any church), or being defined by any one group. But we both appreciate exploring and finding new tools that can help us on our journey.

Essentially, auditing is the re-telling of emotional traumas we have experienced until there is no emotional charge left. When we feel neutral after several repetitions, apparently that experience is filed in the analytical mind instead of the reactive mind. I gave it a whirl to discover if I could achieve the results my friend was having. I notice, after just a few sessions, that events I would previously talk about in an emotional way are now just events. I can speak about or recall these events without pain.

Before I began my auditing sessions, I took a long quiz to establish a baseline of where I am on the emotional scale, love of life, self-love, and much more. The results were not pretty. I've been through some incredibly difficult things in the last couple of years. (*Fast forward about a month. I took this same quiz again and all life areas went up dramatically. I was above the baseline of where I should be on almost every section.*)

As I carry on through this spiritual journey, I notice more and more opportunities to attend spirit-based events, I connect with friends I love dearly more frequently, and clear out emotional aspects of myself that held me back. As Lokpal, one of my spiritual teachers I wrote about earlier once said, "Once you open up, it comes rushing in. You've hooked up to a spiritual I.V.!"

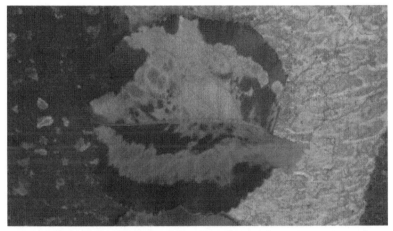

Nature is definitely my greatest spiritual teacher and greatest source of peace.

Keep in mind this all took place in less than one week. And the greatest blessing is I was able to stay at my friend Gary's house. We were attending much of this together and we had a chance to have late night talks catching up with each other. We made conscious how much we appreciate the friendship and how nice it was to have someone to talk to late at night or early morning. This was another affirmation of one of my principles in this book. "Connection" is essential to spiritual growth and happiness (unless someone is a renunciate or choosing to take silent retreat alone).

My blood is now saturated with good authentic friendship experiences, meditation, emotional clearing, and so much more. This week's I.V. was a powerful one!

Current Book – Returned to *On the Road* by Jack Kerouac. (Having a hard time getting through this. It's much darker than what I typically read. The more filled with light I become, the less I can handle anything dark. I'm not relating much to this book, but I'm working on finishing it. Something about not finishing a book seems odd to me.)
Quote of the Day – "Better to sleep in an uncomfortable bed free, than sleep in a comfortable bed unfree." – Jack Kerouac from the book listed above

HELP ME HELP

Day 74 – October 26, 2014 – 7:24 p.m.

Halle-flippin'-lujah! Mercury is out of retrograde. I'm not a huge subscriber to "expecting" things to fail or technology to go wonky. However, when I scan through the various retrogrades in "retro"-spect, often the wonkiness directly lines up.

This past week I had a cough/cold, had to get a new phone, my car was in the shop several times, and I went through periods of not wanting to talk to anyone or apply for jobs over the computer (mercury rules technology and communication).

Thank Goddess I woke with a feeling of fresh air flowing through my soul. I went to visit my cat, Ellie, at my ex's home and dashed up to a healing/DNA activation/channeling in Ojai after dog sitting the most untrained dogs on the planet. Talk about delving into my spirit to keep from locking them in a closet! I was mauled, licked, smacked in the face, and clawed to death. A good time was had by all!

Can you handle that face? Visits with my cat are essential to my soul's happiness. <3

Back to my point(s). The group healing session with my friend was wonderful. At one point she channeled some ascended masters and angels who disconnected unhealthy energetic chords between us and others (living or otherwise). She knows virtually nothing about me and yet did a whole disconnect between myself and two very powerful people in my life whom I have had some painful experiences with. This disconnection of the chord allows for a more healthful flow of energy between people. The dynamics the facilitator picked up on were amazing. She had no idea I had issues with the two people that surfaced. It felt incredibly healing to experience this today.

She did this for about twenty of us and every person recognized who she was bringing up. The more open I am to these healing experiences, the more I attract them. I really resonate with healing work that feels authentic, pure, and truthful to my soul.

I've also switched my focus from bank account balances and "proof" of what's coming in, to a focus on the spirit within. This doesn't mean I'm running around like an illusory hippie in denial (meaning someone who talks all day about what would be ideal but never does anything about it). I'm working on the "doing" as well as the "being." I applied for several jobs online in a moment of feeling aligned. Rather than focusing on the outcomes of my actions, I'm paying close attention to how I feel, and how I'm "being" as I move through various actions. When I feel resistant, I don't apply for work. In fact, I've applied for almost none. Only recently did I have an experience where it felt okay to hop online and send some applications in.

Call it what you like – Spirit, Great Spirit, God(dess), Love, Truth, Inner Voice, Pachamama, Nature, Oneness – I'm healing the Self, the energetic place in me and I am watching how my days are filled with miniature miracles as a result. For example, the gal at the car shop was what I would describe as low on the consciousness scale. There was no way I was going to have any good conversation with her if I started talking about stuff I talk about here on this blog. She was watching Jerry Springer, looking bored, and replied, "Nothing," when I asked her what she liked about working there.

This was a huge opportunity to step into "affinity" and find something we had in common. I began to ask her questions about what she would do with her life if she didn't have to work there. This was done in an approachable way, not a this-crazy-girl-won't-leave-me-the-hell-alone-to-watch-my-shows way. She slowly opened up and showed a piece of her heart to me. She had dreams. She wanted to work with animals. I knew she had been indoctrinated into the harshness of life and her dreams had been stolen from her. She believed her work capacity was making appointments and coffee at a car shop with angry people and a blaring television.

I turned the television to silent. I told her I don't watch television. I continued to listen to her. She drove me to my friend's house since my car needed an overnighter. Her car was filled with candy wrappers, dirt, and random crappy impulse purchases one would find at drug stores such as flashlights in the shape of high heels, dangling tree air fresheners, and gossip magazines. I know she was mad that she had to give me a courtesy lift to my friend's house. She was supposed to be off work and I was an extra trip at the end of a monotonous day. I tipped her (letting go of money when you have nearly none is a great abundance exercise), which she tried to refuse, and I watched her attitude shift as she smiled and told me to have a good day.

Sometimes we can't change anyone's life. They have to change it themselves. But we have a choice how we interact with people and always have the opportunity to show them that someone out there cares about their dreams.

Part of why I feel so aligned this week is because I'm reading *The Abundance Book* by John Randolph Price. I've been meditating on daily concepts for forty nights and it's wonderful! There are major cognitions that surface all day long. One of the most powerful things I've been thinking on is this – **the *consciousness* of Source AS the supply and abundance**. It's not the *effect* of seeing abundance (like money) in my life. Source *is* it. Being conscious of the infinite prosperity of that source is what I choose to do or choose to cut myself off from. But it's my choice. I absolutely love the ability to feel into the prosperity of Source rather than the outcome we search for to prove our abundance. Abundance is an energy, not a monetary amount. Money is one channel through which abundance shows up, but it's not the Source.

It's just so beautiful how my life is moving in this spiritual direction. And it's not some label I made up. I truly am leaving that life I lived, focused on the physical outcomes (and being depressed about it all), and stepping into the heart space instead. I'm listening to how I can use my gifts to be of service. Sometimes it's simply to remind someone that they have the right to continue dreaming.

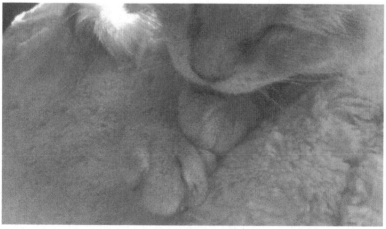

Is there anything more beautiful than a happy kitty?

"Help me help." This is my prayer. I heard this prayer from other spiritual souls throughout my lifetime and I really resonate with it now.

"Help me serve using the gifts I love using!"

Yes! That one feels so good!

What gift(s) would you use to serve this world?

Current Book – *The Abundance Book* by John Randolph Price (This tiny book is incredible. Highly recommend! You'll finish reading it in about twenty minutes. But the magic happens as you do the daily exercises!)
Quote of the Day – "The only problem facing you in life is the belief in separation from your Source. Solve that one and all the other ones will vanish."- John Randolph Price

ADVENTURE IS CALLING!

Day 77 – October 29, 2014 – 3:55 p.m.

Holy guacamole! I watched one of my favorite documentaries ever. A fourteen year old Dutch girl decided to sail a boat (she refurbished herself) around the world to become the youngest girl to ever do this. Let me say that again. *A fourteen year old girl sailed a boat around the world by herself*! I had such a sense of awakening from watching *Maidentrip*. It felt like my soul recognized this girl's soul, her love of nature, her desire to often be alone with her thoughts, her focus, her silence; there was a resonance with her adventurous desires.

I need to start planning and stop "thinking" about doing adventurous things. It could be as simple as riding my bike from San Francisco to Los Angeles. A couple months of training, maximum, would do it. Throw in a route plan and some food with a side of rest spots, and I'd be good to go! I believe this type of trip would be enough of a stretch and also provide a sense of adventure.

I see beauty like this on a regular basis. Adventure courses through my soul!

My life is a daily adventure; don't get me wrong. I see, move, go, play, drive, hike, and explore more than most people. But as far back as I can remember, my soul has had a deep calling to do long pilgrimages (or even short ones). I want to hike the Camino de Santiago trail in Spain. I want to hike the Appalachian Trail (Peace Pilgrim, who hiked this ages ago, is one of my heroes!). I recently learned about a trail through some of our Northern States as well. It's called the North Country Trail. The John Muir Trail speaks to me, and, oh my, so many trails of goodness to enjoy! My heart palpitates when I think about these journeys.

When I was in college, I studied for six months in England. Most days I cut class and said things like, "Welp, I'm off to Scotland. Anyone with me? Or should I hit Wales today instead?"

At one point I hiked Ben Nevis by myself (highest peak in Scotland). The top was covered in falling snow as I approached. I had to turn back a few feet from the top, as I could not find the trail at that point. A bird (who I believe was my grandmother) hopped down the trail, looking back at me to guide me in the right direction until I crossed the white-out area. I'm grateful for these adventures I've had and I seek more of them. I've been hiking on my own since I moved from Chicago to Phoenix in eighth grade. While many of my peers were out partying and having sex, I was communing with the mountains, reading, and being a complete nerd with my friends.

Finding new fruit stands around Ojai is another adventure I love. Especially when I'm on a bicycle!

When I watched *Maidentrip*, I immediately had the thoughts, "I wonder if I could walk the entire edge of Australia? Has anyone done this? How many miles would it be?" And so on. Stuff like this comes to me all the time. I also attract more and more adventure books, info, and movies.

What holds us back? Why do we have a thought that pairs with feelings of excitement and exhilaration and then it fades away within seconds due to the "challenges" our minds immediately come up with? Is the key to simply ignore the challenging thoughts and stick with the passion? Are the true adventurers the ones who ignore the "you can't do that because..." voices? It could be that simple. Forge ahead with a plan. Do step one. Then continue. Step two will arrive. And if we follow this, what will happen? We will do things the fourteen year old girl did. We will achieve our dreams!

Beautiful Ojai persimmons. Another adventure find.

I am so lit up. I am so on fire. There is a deep passion within me burning to go live the adventures that have been kindled in my soul. I could do so much good, so much fundraising, so much awareness with these tours and pilgrimages. I have so much to share and so many ideas pumping through me. This is why I get so frustrated with getting a job. I don't want a flipping normal job. But it takes money to do some of this stuff (or maybe not, but for now I do have some bills and responsibilities to take care of, coupled with an inner knowingness to continue seeking employment).

I will do what I need to for now. I'm in the process of interviewing at a big health food store where I will be the equivalent of an assistant manager in the vitamins/bodycare department. I've done all of this before. This is not a challenge for me. But it would expose me to other naturally-focused people and also to new adventures because it's about six hours north near San Francisco. The Ventura/Ojai area feels a bit dull to me. I'm ready for change. I've hiked masses of trails and spent seven years exploring this area. The thought of being further north amidst the redwoods is very appealing.

Follow your heart into the adventures you dream of!

I'll update you all soon on the job situation, but for now I'm enjoying the adventure. Most people don't have the freedom I have (or don't think they do). Many people have families with kids in school or legal obligations to stay put. I can go anywhere I want. It's just me, my car, and my eager soul.

Here's to the adventures of the future! I hope to see you on my journeys. There will be many.

Current Book – *Following Atticus: Forty-eight high peaks, one little dog, and an extraordinary friendship* by Tom Ryan (I loved this book! Just a man, his dog, and the trails. You'll definitely smile and cry reading this one!)
Quote(s) of the Day – "I was not a religious man, but if I were, the woods would be my church, the mountaintops my altar." (I couldn't resist the following quote as well!) "But that's the thing about

adventures—you're invited to take a chance without knowing the outcome, and all that matters is that you say yes." – Tom Ryan

AWAY AND TOWARD

Day 78 – October 30, 2014 – 5:07 p.m.

This morning's observances were a huge confirmation to leave the Ventura/Ojai area. Ojai is one of (if not my favorite) towns I've ever been to. I love it on so many levels. Ventura, on the other hand, I have never been attached to – other than it's a nice little beach town. It does, however, get more and more inundated with dangerous, transient drug addicts and homeless people (as I've mentioned in earlier blogs).

This morning before nine a.m. I parked near the beach off Seaward. A guy pulled up in a relatively nice Jeep Liberty, pulled out a brown bag with one of those giant beers, turned to the side so people (he thought) couldn't see him, and slammed the whole beer in a few gulps. Then he got up and went to walk the beach with his cigarettes. When I got out of my car, I saw he had prescription pills in his front seat. So he obviously slammed some pills with his breakfast of champions. I debated whether to call the cops and make sure he didn't get on the road, but I just let it go.

A couple parking spots over, a guy pulled in with a fairly nice pick-up truck and for some reason he was buddies with a few red-faced drunkards and drug addicts who swarmed him on their worn out bikes. Two of them got into his truck with a big bag of enough liquor to last the day. And there they sat as I did a phone interview for some work I'm seeking. This all took place within a few moments and all I did was park at the beach for a quiet phone conversation early in the morning.

Sometimes we want to curl up in a ball and turn away from the madness. It's okay.

Why do I tell you all this "negative" stuff and go into the scenarios? For a number of reasons listed below.

- Seeing this stuff is a clear sign to go away. It is helping me detach from where I previously thought I *had* to live (Often we become attached to places versus allowing for change.). Also, by observing my surroundings and sharing my process of releasing attachments, I can help others who are on similar paths, and perhaps do not know how to move ahead.
- Observing this helps us understand the scope of addiction. When we see things like this happening before nine in the morning, maybe it will help us see the huge trap substances can get us into. Awareness is a powerful tool to help us move toward and away from things.

- Whenever we go through an awakening, or a spiritual shift, we will often come up against the things we resist in the world. Because I have a huge past of dating addicts, I'm working on releasing whatever that vibration is within me. I do not connect with the need to numb myself with drugs. It's almost like watching aliens when I see people enjoying drugs or strung out on something. The key, or part of the journey, is to not emotionalize it every time I see it. Can I learn to notice it, turn my back on it, and continue moving in the direction of my dreams? Heck yes! And maybe I can move to a place where I see less of the toxicity. All things are possible.

We can be, do, and have anything we want. We can live where we want. We can *choose* our environment. If you think you can't because of "money" or a "person" or a "condition", start reading anything you can get your hands on that supports your vision and teaches you how to live your dreams. You have been programmed negatively like a computer. Those are *not* your thoughts you think when you dwell on why you can't be, do, or have something. More on that another day; I'm just dropping some seeds into the vast ecosystem of the mind to help you grow some new outlooks! Keep researching until you find the answers you want. They're all within you, but sometimes we have to read, observe, test, reflect, question, and interact with the world around us to find our way in this wild place!

Point yourself toward your next step!

I'm grateful for what I saw this morning. I'm grateful for the juxtaposition of interviewing by phone as I move toward my next dream, and the sad reality of disempowerment just a few cars away. Those folks have as much choice in their lives as I do. I could, this very minute, find some drugs to numb myself out and lessen the pains I've been through, but I choose differently for myself. They, too, can choose recovery. They can choose to focus on pleasure or focus on pain. We are powerful beyond measure and anything that convinces us of anything less is surely not our friend.

I'm your friend. I'm here telling you I support you and believe in you. I'm here, in total belief of 100% of anything you want. Never give up. Never stop choosing better for yourself. I hope by choosing better for myself, by moving away from the toxicity so that I may move toward more beauty – that you will see it's possible. We cannot keep running away without having a better option to move toward. This is part of the key. The "away" part is all that you resist. If I run and run and run away from the toxicity I see, without keeping my mind fixed purposefully on the things that feel better, I'll just be running in circles forever. It's okay to notice what you resist. It will help provide contrast. Then you can create what you want to move toward instead.

Perhaps if you see it's possible, you'll take your own step forward into the possibility of what speaks from deep in your soul. You deserve it. You *are* worthy! You *are* good enough! And you are *very* loved.

Current Book – *Wild: From Lost to Found on the Pacific Crest Trail* by Cheryl Strayed
Quote of the Day – "I knew that if I allowed fear to overtake me, my journey was doomed. Fear, to a great extent, is born of a story we tell ourselves, and so I chose to tell myself a different story from the one women are told. I decided I was safe. I was strong. I was brave. Nothing could vanquish me." – Cheryl Strayed

SMOKED SALMON AND SCIENTOLOGY

Day 81 – November 2, 2014 – 4:39 p.m.

A couple weeks ago my dear friend, Jo, took me to Los Angeles for the day. She wanted to show me the areas she once lived and to enjoy some delicious food as we gallivanted around. Jo and I met at an Ojai networking group and became instant friends. We even started a heart-based networking group that has since dissolved as we went on to do other things. Jo and her husband, Ross, are very dear people to me. I've spent many dinners with them sobbing post-breakup. They let me send my mail to their house when I had none to send it to. My bike and several items are still in storage at their house. We also have been through many incredible trips, lectures, and wild experiences together. I know Jo is my friend, whether we talk three times a week or once every couple months. I'm eternally grateful for her presence in my life, as she is also a personal development junkie and we can philosophize into the long hours of the night! There is nothing better in this world than beautiful meaningful conversations with loved ones, eh?

Our Los Angeles day began with an incredible tour through some posh areas. Los Angeles has always felt like a melting pot of noise and crime to me, but when you explore the nooks and crannies, you find some real gems! The houses were covered in roses. We saw old mansions and new, modern places with sleek lines, fountains, and fantastic combinations of metal and wood. I love modern designs. I love how clean they are. I love the mixture of elements. I'd like a blend of modern design and bright, warm, inviting colors all around.

Jo and I next headed to Canter's famous Jewish deli. I had been hearing about this place for years. As someone who's been raised on an abundance of lox, bagels, and rugelach (Oh my lord. I just had to look up the spelling of rugelach because the only spelling WordPress could suggest was "Rachelle". Obviously, WordPress needs a Jewish update!); I was anxiously awaiting these delights.

My mouth watered as a large platter of extra pickles I ordered arrived. A love of pickles is a bit of an understatement for me. Full sours. None of this half sour crap. A half sour is kind of like a loaf of bread that's been cooked twelve minutes short of done. It tastes like bread. It looks like bread. But you know something is really wrong. There you have it! Pickle philosophy 101 with Jules. I love fermented foods. I've fermented green tomatoes, carrots, celery sticks, cabbage, and hot peppers for hot sauce. Ridiculous. I am a master indeed. I was so mad one year when I had a housewarming party and gave away all my hot sauce and pickled green tomatoes. Dang-it. Now I know better.

Anypoo...

The smoked salmon, white fish, and lox arrived as well. Our eyes were popping out of our heads. You can see below Jo's eyes increased about 400% in diameter. :-)

I took a bunch of photos of the random posters all over the place for my Momela. She loves Jewish everything. If she was closer (she's in Florida), she'd probably live at Canter's. It's delish. Do go.

With full bellies, Jo and I moved on and saw more houses and cool streets around the area. We also admired the Freemasons building. It's truly stunning. Whenever we pass by a building from one of the many Secret Societies (many of them not-so-secret) we always have great discussions about them. People are afraid of the wisdom taught in these societies. For the most part, the wisdom is nothing more than what actually works. You learn the science of how to be, do, and have everything you want. The problem, however, is keeping this information from people, which creates sectors of control.

We also passed by the Hollywood Scientology Center. Because we had both experienced some interesting auditing sessions, we thought it would be wild to take a tour of this gorgeous building and hotel. There were famous people roaming around. Everything was polished and gilded. Men and women in suits greeted us. I felt like I stepped into the Ritz and everyone was there to tend to my every need. This is where it gets good.

One of the attendants showed us around and sat us in a small but astronomically fancy theater. He left us alone in the fancy movie seats to watch a movie about L. Ron Hubbard and Scientology. We were impressed with the beauty and abundance of the place, but also had the giggles. The movie was kind of corny and the experience was similar to being welcomed at a time share. If we're impressed enough, we'll buy! This was completely different from the understated, moldy, run-down Santa Barbara building I went to for auditing. That place was absolutely relaxed and no one tried to get me to do anything. They were just there to be of service each time I arrived for my sessions. This place, however, was very Hollywood-ish.

Jo and I continued to giggle, make fun of the movie, and wondered if we would get ourselves kicked out of the theater. Can you imagine? A nice English gal like Jo and a homeless girl on the front page of the LA Times: *Too much laughing gets two Ojai hippies kicked out of Scientology theater.* We wondered if we should ask for popcorn, but perhaps that would be a little over the top.

At the end of our tour, we sat down with one of the attendants. He said there was a job opening at one of the new Narcanon facilities in Ojai. I told him my background in council (sacred listening circles), personal development, coaching, natural health, etc. and he told us if we came back for a course that night he would introduce us to the guy heading up the Narcanon project. I figured, what the heck? Anything is possible. Perhaps I could serve by helping people heal. He said he would call this gentleman and have him head over in the evening.

By then Jo and I decided to take a two hour course, since the tools seemed to be what we resonated with so far. We went to a nearby park for a while, read a book, relaxed, ate a little dinner, and headed back to the center. Our class was actually really good! It surprised me that I was getting something out of it. I forget the name, but it had to do with working effectively, organizing, eliminating chaos, and moving forward. Jo and I enjoyed it very much and wanted to head out for the night.

As an artist myself, I find this quote to be really lovely.

Of course there was no way the staff was going to show us to the door. They led us back to the room where we first conferenced. There was no mention of the Narcanon gentleman. There were a few staff members with us in the room. The one we'd been dealing with asked us to register for the follow-up course you take from home and email your homework to the teacher. I had about $2.58 in my account. Jo had paid for the class we already took, and I felt very at peace with what I learned. I had no desire to continue in that moment. I told the guy I would not be registering tonight. He gave me some reasons why I should and I told him again. He again did not listen to me and brought me up to the counter to meet one of the other people there. He explained who I was, that I just took the evening course, and perhaps would like to take the continuation of that course.

I looked at this man (and the other two behind the counter) and said, "I will not be taking the next course. I have $2.58 in my bank account and I live in my truck. Perhaps another time."

They both look dumbfounded as if they did not quite understand how I made it there for the first course. I told them Jo gifted me tonight and that if she wants to continue, to speak with her. I told Jo I would not be moving forward with courses.

Jo and I were taken to the "accounting office" or something of that nature. Several people were hard at work. A gentleman sat across from us and got ready to sign Jo up for the course. Before we sat down, the gentleman we originally worked with was sort of whispering something to this man. He seemed to have no understanding that anyone would ever say "no" to him. He leaned in and said, "Let's get you gals going on your next course."

I looked at Jo and then started to laugh. She had said yes to taking the course. I had said no about twelve times. I repeated, yet again, "I will not be continuing with the home course. There is no money in my account to continue."

The guy looked at me, kid you not, and said, "I don't understand."

I would've paid to see a photograph of my face at that moment.

"I have $2.58 in my bank account. And I live in my truck. Jo was kind enough to treat me to the course this evening and she will be continuing on her own."

It took all my strength not to laugh out loud with abandon. Maybe I should have. I certainly did once I got to the car!

There was *never* a mention of the Narcanon guy. No one actually cared about my gifts whatsoever. I was a complete misfit. The people who walk into the Scientology Center are Hollywood people. They have more than $2.58 in their bank accounts. I bet every now and then a homeless person walks in looking for a bathroom and is turned away; but certainly no one from Ojai, on escapade with her home-girl, for the pure pleasure of experiencing the beauty of the building and a random class.

(Fast forward: I've called the Center three times since that day to be taken off their mailing list. They are still sending me gorgeous leaflet invitations to their galas and several magazines a month. Short of calling a lawyer, I don't know how I will actually remove myself from their list. My mom has also received mail from them addressed to me. I have never given her address out to anyone, under any circumstance. I write this here as a service warning to others. Enjoy the tools, read the materials, but only give your contact info out if you are prepared to be constantly hounded with mail.)

I have no issues with tools that feel good. Certain tools created by Hubbard are absolutely genius. Some of his thoughts, or downloads he received, are also genius. I am grateful for the cognitions and healings I've received from the tools I opened up to. But I don't want to be "sold" anything. And I certainly do want to be heard and respected. When someone gives you a clear "no", you respect the "no". If it's not okay to rape someone who says "no", why is okay to attempt a selling rape? Perhaps this is a bit extreme, but I think it's a good question to ask. There are moments when people say "no" and we may inquire to ask why, or to better understand them. Maybe we can improve our businesses by seeking these answers. But to be sold something, several times over, without care or respect of the "no" that's being given is not okay.

This is a great experience that allows me to keep tuning in to my intuition. The tools resonated with me. Scientology as a religion and a community said "no" to me. And that's okay. There's something out there for everyone. One thing I'm very proud of is that I'm not scared to explore, seek out new experiences, and see how they feel for me.

Our day came to an end as Jo and I headed back to Ojai. It was very fun and very different than either of us thought it would be. I think we both expected to go to more shops, perhaps bookstores, coffee houses, quaint places here and there. I guess we have an excuse to go back! Today was quirky and awesome. Just like us! Thank you for a marvelous day, my sweet friend. There will be many more to come.

Current Book – *Wild* by Cheryl Strayed.
Quote of the Day – "The ache for home lives in all of us, the safe place where we can go as we are and not be questioned." – Maya Angelou

NORTHWARD I GO!

Day 98 – November 19, 2014 – 7:04 p.m.

So much has happened since my last entry! I can barely remember it all. For a while I didn't have much internet access, as I was doing some car camping and working here and there.

Then I house sat for some people who have a precious kitty I mentioned in another blog. It was lots of fun and I had a chance to do some odd jobs, relax, unwind, stretch out after sleeping in my car, do laundry, and use the internet.

"Don't mind if I do!"

During the time I was there, I was in contact with someone about a job just south of San Francisco. I'm not going to mention the name of the company, as I currently work there and also it's not about ostracizing people. This is just about the experience of entering back into the corporate world. I drove up and back in one day (six hours each way) to interview and they called a day or two later to say I got the job working as the equivalent of assistant manager in vitamins and body care. This is all stuff I used to do when I managed a similar department

147

years ago at Sunflower Market; not terribly challenging, but enough to present some consistent income as I build this business and also a chance to move locations.

The photo above is untouched. When I interviewed for my new job, this tree seemed to be glowing and beckoning me there!

I have been craving the redwood trees and getting into new areas where there is some rain sometimes (ha). Ojai is sunny almost every day which I do love, but is experiencing major drought. It is refreshing to have rain and see greenery even though I truly do love to sun worship! I also wanted to get into a very conscious area and there's a big progressive movement going on up north and lots happening. I think I will have more access to clients and community. Ojai shall remain in my heart forever!

As of now, I cannot afford to get a place or even rent a room for that matter (A very inexpensive studio apartment in a questionable neighborhood is about $1,500 per month here). My credit bills, car insurance, gas, food, etc. are the equivalent of a high rent as it is. So I will stay in my car, join a gym to shower, and save up for a place.

Besides, I really have loved the adventure and camping in my car truly feels amazing on some nights, especially those when I am under the stars in a quiet area and I can watch the moon come up. I need to search out good places to stay here that are safe. For now I will stay on a road in a quiet dark neighborhood where it *feels* safe. I would prefer to see the moon, though!

Grabbing water at Bonny Doon Spring

I landed last night up here after taking my time driving. I began the trip a night ahead of time, slept halfway at a rest area, and then took my time coming up Highway 1 from Santa Cruz. I stopped at Bonny Doon Spring and spent almost two hours collecting spring water. (Collecting spring water takes me to an indescribable place in my soul. I feel an instant connection to Mother Earth and could collect water for endless days.) The spring ran as a slow drip, so I seized the opportunity to do my *Abundance Book* exercise and look at trees while I waited. The water has a tds (total dissolved solids) level of only 55! That's fantastic for wild water! Very pure, indeed. It tastes magnificent. A little minerally, but barely. So blessed!

As I drove through the hills, smelled the redwoods, and hiked the cliffs near Half Moon Bay, it certainly felt like coming home to a new place, yet familiar. These places call me. They are in my DNA. They are part of my soul!

I ran into a book, *Blue Mind*, about the science of why living by water makes life better. Can't wait to read that! I I also picked up an organic chocolate covered strawberry truffle and smelled the salt air. I watched the white speckled seals. While watching a gorgeous sunset from Half Moon Bay, I ate clam chowder. I also had a strange feeling in my gut as I passed from the coast into the crowded city where I will work. It's so busy and packed there. The town is nice. There are lots of great restaurants and opportunities, but still not my ultimate choice of where to live. I really feel deeply in my soul that I want land near water with big trees – coast, rivers, streams, redwoods, and a mild climate, warm in summer, cool in winter with no snow, which is essentially where I am, but closer to the ocean than the city. As I save money, I will look into land for sale that I could one day build on and will have access to spring or well water.

Last night I parked in town not far from work, on a cute little street. I slept well from about 8:30 p.m. to 6:00 a.m. and then got up to search out a restroom. Everything is simple and complicated all at once when you live in a car. Driving to a bathroom that is open at the crack of dawn is complicated. Not paying rent or having a house to clean is simple. It all balances. There are pros and cons to both.

Despite needing a shower pretty badly, I headed into work for my first day of orientation. Seeking out a gym will be the next mission so I can clean up a bit. Baby wipes are not exactly a shower (or shampoo). Luckily I'm clean enough that no one would guess I spent the last couple of nights sans bathing.

It's interesting to note that when I left Ojai, I said goodbye to some buddies and it was clearly harder on them than it was on me. I was so ready for change and adventure that it was incredibly smooth to move on. It did not feel sad at all. I think it's often harder to be left than to do the leaving, emotionally. I do have dear friends for life I treasure in my heart. I know we will remain friends and continue to see one another, regardless of distance. My heart thumped for the people I was leaving more than it did for myself. I understood how they felt. It also makes me incredibly grateful to notice how many deep connections and friendships of meaning are all around me. For this I am infinitely grateful. The hardest part of leaving was having to kiss my little kitty, Ellie Belle, goodbye. While I am eternally happy she is in the great care of my ex, I miss her every day. Our bond runs deeper than I ever thought it would.

My next blog will continue with the journey of landing in my new "home" along this spiritual journey and the hilarity of my first day of work. Stay tuned!

Current Book – *Wild* by Cheryl Strayed
Quote of the Day – "I'm a free spirit who never had the balls to be free." – Cheryl Strayed

CORPORATE CHUCKLES

Day 98 – November 19, 2014 – 7:36 p.m.

This is my second entry in one day. My last entry got long and I decided to end it where I embarked on my first day of work in my new town.

Today was full of hysterical laughter (in my mind). After working for myself or small private companies for so many years, it was insane to go back to corporate culture. The gal who was training us on the graces of "social appropriateness in our professional environment" used several valley girl abbreviations that did not remotely sound professional. I think I heard the word "totes" (totally), "perf" (perfect), and "hella" (very, lots of) at least three or four times during my orientation today. This is not to say that my "trainer" is anything less than a wonderful, lovely person. She's great and I respect her. But it was a very odd and funny experience to be lectured on what's professional amidst the lack of professional things happening. Not only was I smothered in Bay Area slang, I also had to sit and wait for about a half hour beyond my start time because no one was ready to train me. Leaders are on time. Professionals speak with a very conscious choice of words. This was like entering The Twilight Zone.

When I leave work, I focus on the beauty all around me.

153

It's amazing how serious this company takes itself, the rigorous interview I had to do, the many people I had to call ahead of time to "reach out and do my due diligence", yet people are late, my questions are only half answered, and not one person said hello to me at the store except one happy looking hippie. I've been told repeatedly how important the culture, the friendliness, and customer service are, but no one ever introduces themselves to me. I always introduce myself. Another gal came to do paperwork and plopped down on the chair with her computer to have us enter info. She didn't even say her name. So I asked. What's funny is that I am being told how fabulous the "culture" of this company is, but everything I see is just a bunch of conditioned corporate people who seem relatively bored and dispassionate. I recognize this is only my first day of work, but I did come up to interview for the day and had about eight phone conversations before being hired. The typical corporate "blah" came through most of the conversations I had and I talked to very few people who sounded like they authentically liked what they did for a living. I was not surprised. It just did not seem congruent with everything I had been told about this company. When you work in personal development and with people who are very passionately invested in their lives, their work, and who are filled with positive slants on everything, it's truly like stepping back into the Stone Age to experience corporate life.

Another chuckle arose in my mind when we were taken on a store tour. Our trainer walked us over to the salad bar to sample some food. Before I could even put a lone strip of cabbage in the sample cup, the gal took off calling us. It was straight out of a Saturday Night Live clip. I felt like a bag lady, trying to hold my paperwork, backpack, and a trail of cabbage that didn't make it into the cup lest I be late for the next part of our tour. Thus, I chuckled to myself again.

Hilariousness continued. We walked around each department and were given samples to take home of food, body care, and more. The whole time we were told corny stuff about why this food is the best. Then the trainer started pulling private label products off the shelf. After a brief health lesson (much of which was incorrect), she added, "And remember. We're of course keeping in mind how we love our quality store brand."

Was I watching a tampon commercial? It sure felt like it. Products were being held up to the face, fake smiles were being produced, and seductive lingo was thrown up all over us in hopes we would love our quality store brand. It's not that our store brand isn't full of quality ingredients (for the most part). It was the selling of it to people who were already sold. Um...I spoke with about eight people about the fantastic nature of the company. I don't think I need to be sold on private label spaghetti. I almost couldn't contain myself. It was like I was watching a commercial and someone was selling me something I already bought years ago. I already shop here. No one needs to "sell me" on our brands. I left there feeling like I just went to a training at any mainstream corporate fast food chain even though we are apparently one of the most progressive companies in the nation to work for. I also felt a bit like I used to on school field trips. A teacher would be puking up facts about something as I stared into the distance, wishing the day would end so I could go home and play in the garden.

Later I went to a fitness place to seek out membership info (to shower and use the sauna and maybe a treadmill). Let me stress the word *info*. The gal wanted to lecture me and also wanted to ask me a million questions about my needs and desires, my weight and health goals (in order to make the sale). I stopped her, told her she was doing an awesome job and that I have done similar commission work before. I told her I understand how sales pitches work, why she needs to get me in the computer now rather than later - but I won't be buying a membership tonight.

Next I shared with her that I want to check out some places on my own and likely will come back the next day. She kept pushing and pushing. It was very uncomfortable and I know I came off like a hard ass to her because she was young and still innocent in the ways of sales.

Regardless of what I would say, she would begin asking me the same set of questions or arguing with the fact that I wanted to look other places. She also wanted to know what those places were so she could sell me on why her place was better. While I understand she was entirely convinced that she was doing her job, I was trying to help her understand that she wasn't listening to what the client needs. I was asking for basic gym membership pricing. I clearly expressed my needs for a shower, sauna, and very minor gym use (I like to hike and be outdoors instead of a gym). I wanted to be left alone, as an intelligent shopper and human being, and to make an empowered choice after looking at my options.

Amidst the structures, we can still be free!

After over an hour of talking, I was able to get this employee talking about starting her own business, her family from Mexico, and meditation (which she does not yet do but her boyfriend does). In the end, I think she felt better but at first I know she just felt like I was a client with a wall up.

What's funny is my wall was down and I was entirely transparent. I stated up front that she need not waste her time and to let me move forward, as I am very intelligent and capable of choosing the right gym for myself. This is another hilarious example of someone conditioned by the corporate model of sales. (We are taught to put the company's needs before the client's needs.) One of the biggest problems we have these days is we assume our consumers are dumb (This is a topic I've touched on before and will continue to touch on it, as it informs so much of how we do business.) Tap into the consciousness of this assumption. How does that feel for you? Do you want someone to assume you know nothing and approach you in this way? Or would you rather be approached as if you are a magnificent and divine intelligent being and spoken to with respect and inquiry about your needs? This is a revolutionary process. Here's a great example of the direction I'd like to see us move toward:

Imagine if you went to buy a car and the dealership assumed you were intelligent enough to purchase something at a single, transparent, fair price. Imagine you didn't need to play games such as going back and forth to the dude in the high desk with the sunglasses on making offers until you take the bid? What if they assumed you did your research and know that such and such a car costs $20,000 and therefore you came in and could buy it for that price?

What if we assumed that our prices were so fair that instead of making them $19.99 with a line slashed through them and the new price of $14.99 below it, we just sold it for $14.99, period? Especially when that product **never** sells for $19.99; it's just a psychological game. Is this spiritually aligned? Where does this practice come from? Does it come from honesty? Is it transparent? Are we alright if we sell 9 out of 20 customers the $14.99 instead of 10 out of 20 customers with the price slashed? Or do we need silly tricks to keep people engaged? Maybe all it would take to rise above all the nonsense tactics is for a few revolutionaries to mark prices their actual value without gimmicks. Why is that "insane" to most of the world? Because we allow it to be!

I'm no longer interested in dealing with corporate sales people who do not listen to me. I was brainwashed into thinking I "owe them" my time and need to listen to them for hours. Now I just choose to see past all the tactics and laugh. When you see it for what it is, it's hilarious! The girl at the gym was trying to sell me personal training sessions and insisted that I walk over to the personal trainer wall. I told her I will not be buying sessions (I had no money in the bank for these.) and that I did not want to hear about the sessions. She replied, "But you don't know that you won't want sessions eventually."

Actually, I did know. I knew I would never buy personal training sessions in a place that did not listen to me. And she proceeded to tell me why their sessions are the best and I proceeded to laugh.

Oh lordy, I am off on a tangent about authentic business now. But hey! You've arrived on a site about being on a spiritual journey, and for me that includes every little nuance, from the way I do business, to the way I perceive how others do business, to how I can effect change in a mainstream gym rat. One day she may just realize how powerful she is without the need to "sell" people. I'm not writing all of this to point fingers and make people look small. I'm calling people to think differently about what they automatically accept. Empowerment comes from looking clearly at the situations in front of us and making a choice from our guts. How can we listen to our intuition if we haven't learned to see the true, clear picture of things?

I am sure I will get a gym pass soon, likely tomorrow (I think I can go one more day without being too stinky to be allowed at work. Ha!). And I am sure I will see her again and perhaps keep reflecting to her the possibilities of where she can go in her consciousness. Now to figure out how to get her a meditation track since she didn't give me her email address.

I'm exhausted. Time to sign out of Starbucks and find a place to sleep. I am like an old granny and crash around eight or nine every night now as it's dark by 6:30 p.m. or earlier. I know. Total rebel. Blogging at Starbucks with a decaf. Try to contain yourself. I know this is likely the most revolutionary night you could ever imagine (wink wink).

Here's to the many mind chuckles I am sure this new "work" will provide. As I always say, it's hilarious to get a job you don't want. The mission is to no longer *need* the job, thus releasing it and stepping into the purpose(s) we came to gift the world with. Until then, I shall keep on chuckling!

Quote of the day – "Authentic marketing begins not with tactics or strategy, but with the self." – Fabienne Fredrickson

HUGGING AMMA THE SAINT

Day 102- November 23, 2014

Although all aspects of life intertwine and separation is merely an illusion, it's been said that a spiritual life is kindled at a specific point (or points). I feel I've had many kindlings. A woman in my past was the first person to allow for my intuition and taught me about vibration. That was one experience of the light being kindled. There are too many similar moments to count, but in a certain way, along the spiritual thread that courses through me, yesterday was the first day of my life. As one of the women giving service at Amma's world peace ceremony I attended said, "Amma wants you to know that if you receive a mantra, buckle in!"

This woman implied that we would be in for quite a ride. After a long and bumpy number of years, I was hoping for a bit of calm. But I understand this movement is about self-realization, growth, and awakening. So that feels fantastic! How did I arrive at an ashram receiving my first mantra from a hugging saint? It's a bit of a story, so hang in there with me.

A couple of years ago I had no idea who Amma was. Her full name is Sri Mata Amritanandamayi Devi (Amma is a term for Mother). People around me would say things like, "I can't get together this weekend. I'm going down to L.A. to get a hug from Amma. She's in town."

I figured Amma was some type of guru. Because I've never been drawn to going down a single path and attaining a guru, I never looked further into these hugging events. However over the last year or so I watched a few of the "Amma Hugging the World" videos. I also watched some lectures on compassion she did. I immediately felt the shakti go through me and began to sob uncontrollably, regardless of what I was watching. Lokpal, one of my spiritual teachers, told me at the time that I likely found my guru. After looking more deeply into what a guru is, I had less resistance, as it's not at all about choosing a single path and never straying. Freedom is an inherent aspect of a spiritual path with a guru, so I felt a huge sense of relief come over me. I also knew I would one day hug this beautiful soul.

San Mateo bridge view on my way to see Amma.

I had no idea during the last year of sobbing to Amma videos that one of her ashrams was about forty-five minutes from my new job. A couple days ago a friend of Lokpal called me to let me know Amma's schedule. As it turned out, she was going to be at her San Ramon ashram just three days after I started my work here. Amma was holding a free evening world peace ceremony called Devi Bhava with darshan to follow (Her darshan, or blessing, is hugs to all who are willing to wait in line.). Despite just starting work, I magically had yesterday off.

Because I'm anal-retentively early, I left late in the morning and headed across the bay to San Ramon. There was no parking at the ashram, as the current retreaters took over the place. I had to park about four miles away at a business building. I waited for hours until the droves of people showed up. We waited in huge lines and several private "taxis" filled with Amma's followers caravanned us up to the ashram. The people I rode with were all from Grass Valley. We shared a few words and they gave me very intense looks of knowingness that I was in for a real treat. They had all experienced darshan before.

As we lined up, I split off from the group to stand in the "Never been to Amma" line. First timers don't have to wait as long. How cool! The ashram was set in a nest of hills. Hoards of people giving service were cooking massive pots of curry, vegan pizza, and samosas. I purchased the most delicious potato samosa imaginable and listened to the people around me. I was alone but certainly not lonely. It felt very special to be there alone and not "need" anyone to make my time pass or to feel secure.

Waiting teaches patience!

162

Two men behind me discussed spirituality and not wanting to pay for spiritual events. This event was free. There was no obligation to pay a cent, however donations are accepted. If you see the kind of shifts Amma is making with the funds that are donated, you would never question giving money. She's quite revolutionary when it comes to service. For more info about her service work, visit her website at https://www.amritapuri.org/.

A feisty lady behind me also complained. She was upset that the vegan pizza didn't have vegan cheese on it. I just took it all in. Just because I was at an ashram does not mean everyone was mentally at the ashram. Some were still in a place of resistance, having no idea they were living the opposite teachings of Amma (gratitude, compassion, peace, etc.).

Delicious vegan samosa!

I smiled to myself, enjoyed the smell of homemade chai, and noticed how completely content I felt. There was a deep peace within me as I stood "alone" among thousands of people, needing nothing and enjoying everything. I found a lucky penny that morning after sending my friend Randee a message that I was seeing Amma. The synchronicities continued as one would expect. I stood in line for a couple of hours. Then I walked in line to the temple and asked the attendant if it would help if I fill a space up front since I was alone. He said there was one empty seat left. Yes!

I sat next to a young gal with pretty eyes and beautiful lips. She said, "Lucky girl!" as I climbed over her to sit down. I smiled, sharing with her my journey of ending up here after many months of videos and sobbing. She described the power of these events and then said she was from Grass Valley! Seriously? Another one out of these hoards of people? I must need to visit that place.

As I waited for Amma about three rows from the stage (I know! So amazing!), I began to get emotional. I thought about my Dad (he had a stroke a couple of years ago), my ex, my friends, and so much more. I watched the film screen showing Amma's service projects and cried. The tears came and came again. Amma has a way of awakening my heart chakra. Just a simple smile or glace, or even thinking of her often causes me to sob. I'm even crying right now at a coffee house as I journal and charge my phone.

Amma spoke in her native language and a gentleman translated full stories back to us. One story that sticks out is the story of how our minds behave. Amma said it's kind of like when we lose a tooth our tongue constantly goes to the loss, but never did that before we lost our tooth. Now the tooth is gone and the tongue searches and reminds itself of what's missing. The lesson being - not to allow the mind to do the same. Be always in a state of gratitude, noticing what we *do* have.

(Note – no photos allowed during the ceremony out of respect, so the following photos are general nature ones that I feel capture the energy I experienced!)

There was also a story of a man who was given a bag of coins and was told that if he says three words it will multiply infinitely. After the man was told the second word, the other guy who gave him the coins died. The man with the money loses each of his coins. On his last one he is sad because he doesn't have the last word to replenish the coins. A beggar comes along needing money for the children. Since the money will not be resupplied, the man gives away his last coin. In doing so his bag instantly fills. The lesson on giving away your last coin is one taught in many faiths, as so many of us fear loss versus appreciating what we have to give.

I sat and chanted. The holy water Amma blessed was passed around. I added it to my water bottle to infuse it.

After the ceremony we all scattered so the musicians could sit up front while Amma gave darshan. We received tokens, which indicated an order to line up for a hug. As I sat in line someone handed me a card asking if I wanted to receive a personal mantra from Amma. I knew I did. I knew it was meant to be. They said to simply ask her for a mantra and she will understand. My heart began to beat faster and faster as I sat on stage, moving seat by seat closer to her, watching people receive hugs. (It's truly remarkable how thousands of people are organized to avoid any chaos in the hugging process. Also, many people are not aware that Amma does not leave until every person has received a hug. She has hugged people overnight without breaks for food, restroom, or anything else.)

The lights were bright and hot on stage. Everything smelled of roses and mild incense. Loads of devotees helped guide us from seat to seat to meet Amma. I was no longer crying as I walked up to her. There was a sense of overwhelm, almost like I could not shed tears because I was in another state of consciousness. Someone behind me gently pressed my face toward Amma's shoulder to let me know I could hug her now and Amma pulled me in to her right side. I felt her sounds in her chest, I smelled roses, I heard her talking, and then suddenly her returned embrace, kissing the side of my head and face. She cradled me and I said over and over, "Thank you, Amma."

Then I asked, "Can I have a mantra please?"

She gave me a card and I was whisked off the stage. I did not know I needed to go through a process first to receive a mantra. I read the card which said I must receive a mantra orientation on the other side of the stage. A group of us sat in a circle as we chose a personal word that invokes the divine when we think of it. The lady explained that we should not get a mantra from Amma unless we know we want to enter into a sacred contract as a devotee of sorts with Amma. She said mantras are very sacred and powerful and we are to do three things daily:

1. Chant our mantra.
2. Connect with Amma any way we possibly can as much as possible (through photos, videos, etc.)
3. See every person I meet *as* Amma.

The last one was huge for me. It really hit me like a slap in the face. "See every person *as* Amma." The awakening is about seeing the good in all beings, knowing regardless of their choices, the truth is love. I knew I still wanted a mantra. A few people changed their minds and left. My heart felt even closer to Amma as I thought of receiving my mantra. We were instructed to wait in a different line near the stage and wait to be called. Then we were to sit on her right side, facing the crowd. In between Amma's hugs, she would lean back to her devotees who helped her with the mantra process. I gave my word that represented the divine to one of the gentleman helpers and Amma leaned back to hear it in her native language. Based on what she hears, she delivers a different mantra to each person. Amma whispered my mantra in my ear as she leaned back and held me close. I remember her deep voice, the Sanskrit words. The guy behind her handed me the written mantra to practice after she spoke it.

I was not to repeat my mantra to others. It was mine forever. I was so overwhelmed with gratitude. I left the stage and walked upstairs to a small room past hundreds of chanting bodies. A man pronounced my mantra for me properly to help me learn it. The meaning was also explained to me.

I returned to watch Amma a bit more. The men who chant next to her have bone-tingling voices - especially her main devotee who translates for her. His voice takes me back to a primal place in my soul and I feel a sense of oneness when he speaks or sings.

After watching Amma and enjoying the bliss everywhere, I left to purchase a couple of photos in the discount tent. I had to work fairly early the next morning or else I would have stayed and chanted all night, watching the amazing darshan service.

"Total unconditional love and bliss" only touches the tip of the iceberg. I felt that and so much more. Amma says, "My religion is love." Agreed! That's what I feel and why I don't mind having a "guru" on some level. This whole journey is about love, growth and openness. It's not about adopting religious beliefs and rules. I read in one of Amma's books that she's never read any of the Hindu doctrines. She's simply a conduit for love. I relate to this so deeply.

I took a caravan back to my car and believe it or not one of the people in my caravan up to the ashram was with me on the return. What are the chances? I've learned not to question chance anymore. These small synchronicities and divine happenings can't *not* happen when we are in the zone! When we pay attention to our internal guidance system, a trail of very clear signs, confirmations, and happenings will arrive. I'm so glad I listened to my gut when it said to receive a hug from Amma today. I was wavering back and forth, at which point Lokpal emailed me and said, "Do not miss Amma."

And I did not.

Current book – *Amma: Healing the Heart of the World* by Judith Cornell
Quote of the day – "Only when human beings are able to perceive and acknowledge the Self in each other can there be real peace." – Amma

UNIVERSAL HUGS

Day 110 – December 1, 2014

My last blog entry shared my experience of hugging Amma, the saint. That experience was a complete activation of the heart chakra for sure. Since then, many beautiful things have happened and the synchronicities continue. I call these beauties "universal hugs".

My lucky number is 34. It follows me everywhere. Or perhaps I follow it. I'm sitting in my car journaling about several experiences post-Amma. A guy pulled up in a land management truck and his trailer had two giant 34's spray-painted on it. What are the chances? I keep receiving little gifts like this. Some people either do not notice these things, or think they are nothing more than chance occurrences. I find they happen at very precise moments when I desire confirmation or when I am feeling particularly "on path". They feel like a huge hug from the energetic field all around me. It is indeed my choice to view them as something more than senseless and meaningless happenings. And with this choice comes an increase of their occurrences. Obviously, this is a simple law of attraction phenomenon. Focus of attention grows that which is focused upon.

A very "random" trailer with my lucky number on it twice!

After leaving the ashram last week, I had to drive about an hour back to where I work. This requires crossing the San Mateo Bridge. At the toll booth, I smiled at the lady who took my toll fee. I saw her *as* Amma. This was one of the things we learned when we received our mantra, to remember that Amma is in all of us. We can choose to see and feel that love vibration in all of humanity. This is one of my greatest challenges, especially when coming across very toxic people. I must remember they, too, were once a tiny infant no different from me. Several things occurred in their paths to create them into the people they currently are. But the truth within them is the pure light, the pure child, the pure love vibration. When I smile and connect with someone in this pure way, I feel the universe hugging my heart, letting me know I'm looking through the "right" lens.

The day after my Amma experience, I woke before daylight to create time to meditate and recite my mantra before work. *Every* time I thought of Amma or said my mantra, I began to cry. I would see her face, full of light around it, coming to me as I said my mantra or meditated. I was in a perpetual state of gratitude, compassion, love, and emotional release from November 22nd when I received my mantra, until a day or two ago (which was kind of a challenge at work because I couldn't be a sobbing train wreck there).

The second day after hugging Amma, I was sitting on a bench on the Bair Island lookout point. Again tears and love overcame me. My ex's face also came to me over and over as I felt deep love and compassion. I felt as if my mantra was purifying and healing the wounds and reinstating an energy of love between us (not romantically). It's been interesting, as I don't "try" to think of my ex. She just automatically comes to me, here and there.

As I sat meditating on the bench, I opened my eyes and a pelican had swooped down very close to me. Each time I opened my eyes a new bird arrived such as a snowy egret or a full flock of gossipy chicks. I had given the word "nature" to Amma when receiving my mantra (She requests a word we choose that most instantly connects us to the divine. Then our mantra is given in response to this.). Because my mantra must be deeply connected to nature, I began to see more and more evidence of this throughout my meditations. I felt Amma there with me on that bench. I felt her deeply in my heart. Sometimes I cry out of complete bliss and love for Amma, myself, my life, nature, beauty, etc....

I love watching the tide arrive in the bay just before sunrise!

Those are a few of my experiences since my visit with Amma. They tend to happen more frequently. There are too many instances to list in one blog, but I will continue to journal and focus upon the wonderful happenings, thus growing the universal hugs! In fact, I'm sending a great big wish for a universal hug to greet you on your path when you most need it!

Current book – *Amma: Healing the Heart of the World* by Judith Cornell
Quote of the Day – "Love is our true essence. Love has no limitations of caste, religion, race, or nationality. We are all beads strung together on the same thread of love. To awaken this unity and to spread to others the love that is our inherent nature is the true goal of human life." – Amma

CROWS AND MANTRAS

Days 114-132 – December 5-23, 2014

This blog summarizes the last couple of entries in my spiritual/meditation journal. It's been quite the wild ride since receiving darshan from Amma.

December 5, 2014 – I meditated yesterday and did my mantra at the preserve along Shoreline Drive. The juxtaposition of NASA, the Google buildings, and the calm San Francisco Bay was so odd. I typically like to be away from busy areas while enjoying nature, but this is not always possible. I do my best to seek out the special quiet spots in between the madness.

During my mantra practice, a giant black crow flew down and squawked at me so loudly I had to open my eyes and look to my right. It was about 15-20 feet away and there were no other birds surrounding it. The sound was sharp and alarming, as if it arrived to warn me of something. It seemed to purposefully lift me out of meditation so I would see it. After about a minute the crow flew off and I resumed my mantras. Over and over my mantra work is affirmed through nature (Remember…"nature" is the word I gave to Amma signifying my connection with the divine in order to receive my mantra!).

Here are just a couple of the winged friends I've run into lately!

December 12, 2014 – Today's mantra meditation was filled with more crying. As you read in previous blogs, Amma has the ability to go straight to my heart center and I often weep as I meditate, recite my mantra, or recall Amma's face. I also had very vivid visions of a time I punched the outer wall of my home, which I wrote about in this book introduction. There was an ungodly amount of physical and emotional pain at that time and today's meditation session seemed to purify a bit of that out of my system.

Another thing that continues during meditation is having visions of my ex. I wrote about this in the last blog and it's continued since then. I'm not sure why her frequency comes to me. Perhaps it's nothing more than the need to cleanse, heal, and purify. It doesn't feel like a negative thing. It just gets a bit emotional at times.

I'm still seeing masses of crows as well. While eating lunch a couple days ago, a crow swooped down to a branch above me and began to yell for a minute or two before leaving. Again, it was a loud warning-like sound and I felt as if I was being given a message. This was on a very busy street outside work where crows are not often hanging out.

Adorable mushrooms poking their heads up to enjoy the view with me :-)

December 23, 2014– I was reading a book about Amma's life story today at the library, during which I had visions of learning more about Indian spirituality, where Amma grew up, the eastern Gods and Goddesses, and much more. Right after having these impressions I turned to the left and there was a book called "India" sitting on the shelf. It was among other historical books but as I looked over, my eyes went immediately to it. I don't feel compelled right this moment to delve into eastern spirituality, but perhaps this is a confirmation of my deeper learning and growth as I continue this spiritual journey.

My mind was a little more still this morning as I did my mantra meditation. This feels good to approach a stiller place after so many "thoughts" and "visions" which bring so much overwhelming emotion.

Always pause at a goose crossing!

There is so much I'm learning through the commitment to meditate and create a true spiritual practice. This is not to say that we're not all spiritual beings, living the spirit of who we are at all times. But making the choice to commit to a true spiritual practice (or ritual) can increase our awareness, connect us to our inner truth, cleanse and purify, and create a sense of peace. Is it any "accident" that most of our great spiritual warriors spoke of meditation on some level?
Here are the quantifiable things I'm grateful for as a result of meditating these last few weeks:

- Arriving at stillness (After working in a busy, crazy environment five days a week, this is heavenly!)

- Connecting with crows and other animals (If I was reading, watching a movie, or on the computer, my experience of these great creatures would not have happened.)
- Feeling emotion. My heart has a physical sensation when I think of Amma or when the meditations are purifying past occurrences. Creating the space for these feelings and healings is definitely a blessing.
- "Hearing" blog ideas or other projects I want to do. Often during or after meditation, I'll "hear" the words I need to write in order to share with you. Or a new idea for a project will pop into my head.

I'm sure there are other benefits not listed, but that's a pretty dang good start of a list! I wonder what *you* would experience by committing to some sort of meditation practice for the next seven days. If you do commit, consider journaling what your benefits are and then encourage someone else to do the same.

Current Book – *Amma: Healing the Heart of the World* by Judith Cornell
Quote of the Day – "You are a cosmic flower. Om chanting is the process of opening the psychic petals of that flower." – Amit Ray

BI-LOCATION AND THREE CONSCIOUSNESSES

Day 127 – December 18, 2014 – 12:28 p.m.

My life, since leaving Ojai, seems to culminate into two polarities. As you know, I moved up to the peninsula a bit south of San Francisco and attained work in a health food company doing some management work. It's amazing working with customers again, being face to face with someone I can be of service to when they don't know what to buy or help them in their quest for health. (I'm also a little obsessed with the smell of coconut, so now I have access to loads of natural body care with coconut on a daily basis. Heavenly!) Then I leave the crazy crowds at work and melt into almost constant, quiet alone time. Most people come home to televisions, noise, the voices of children, or a roommate or two. I rarely hear anything beyond the sounds of nature, traffic, my own thoughts, or some coffee house music.

Redwood trees through my rainy car window.

We've had pretty major rains the last couple weeks. Some of my favorite moments since moving into my car include listening to the fat raindrops hit the roof in the middle of the night, walking the miles of trails that are minutes from work, doing my daily mantra and meditation practice, and reading voraciously.

This morning I noticed something very interesting. I was holding my mala beads, reciting my mantra as I passed over each bead. At one point my mouth kept saying the mantra *out loud* while my mind was thinking about nature, work, and a number of other things. Then my mind was noticing that it was thinking of other things *while* I was saying my mantra. Which brought me to an important question – Who is saying the mantra, who is thinking of life, and who is observing the two simultaneously take place? At one point there were three active "consciousnesses" perceiving everything. And perhaps a fourth consciousness noticing that all three were taking place. That part I am not entirely sure of. But I know for sure three consciousnesses were actively speaking at the exact same moment.

This brought me to the awareness of our limitlessness. Who, specifically, each consciousness was, on each individual level, was not quite as important to me as the knowingness that if we can operate on three systems that transmit vibrations at once, can we not place each of these "selves" where we want them at any time? This, I believe, may be one key to bi-location. I've been reading *Autobiography of a Yogi* by Paramahansa Yogananda and he shares a story about observing bi-location with a guru who places himself in two places. Two people saw him each place at the same time, and later they shared their experience. This story had a powerful *energetic* effect on me and through that, I am attracting not only experiences that bring up this subject, but also one of my mentors asked me to bi-locate the other day to receive healing from afar while I was working. (No one *ever* talks to me about bi-location. Yet all of these experiences suddenly happen one after the other. Good 'ole Law of Attraction, baby!)

My spirit being grows and grows as I open to and travel deeper into this spiritual journey. I've asked the universe for more wisdom and more experiences that will help me expand into my greatest potential. There is a great peace I feel, and within that an extreme yearning to learn, to expand, to ascend, to live the best life I possibly can. And the gratitude I feel lately is overwhelming. Thank you for sharing this journey with me! Perhaps one of our consciousnesses will bi-locate and visit one another soon.

Current Book – *Unbroken* by Laura Hillenbrand (I'm very sensitive to violence or anything negative. I'm therefore very careful of what I allow into my consciousness. This book was recommended to me and the main thing to gain from it is the triumph of the great human spirit within all of us. Should you choose to purchase this book, note that it's quite the painful journey. Tread lightly.)

Quote of the Day – "Though all three men faced the same hardship, their differing perceptions of it appeared to be shaping their fates. Louie and Phil's hope displaced their fear and inspired them to work toward their survival, and each success renewed their physical and emotional vigor. Mac's resignation seemed to paralyze him and the less he participated in their efforts to survive, the more he slipped. Though he did the least, as the days passed, it was he who faded the most. Louie and Phil's optimism, and Mac's hopelessness, were becoming self-fulfilling." – Laura Hillenbrand from the book sited above

TRUST IN THYSELF

Day 127 – December 18, 2014 – 12:56 p.m.

My last blog post was written the same day as this one. I've been writing up a storm lately! The two topics were separated and I had the sense this one was filled with a message I know someone out there will benefit from!

I've been predominantly watching, listening, and taking things in over the last month. This has been very wonderful for my soul and a great opportunity to stay quiet, check in with my intuition, and continue to live from my gut instinct.

This morning I had a meeting with one of my past mentors online. He was asking me if I was going to come back to our mastermind group I had left due to affordability a few months ago. He's also doing a big challenge online and giving away money to participants and much more. It's a fantastic program. The external voices would assume I am an idiot for not "getting back in". But what I've noticed since I left a few months ago is I have been laser focused, attracted a job quickly, eliminated any need for credit cards, and have seen and done more than many people do and see in years. I've been extremely happy. I could go back to the group, however this would put me under some financial pressure again and I need new tires, an oil change, a new phone (dropped and cracked it a week or more ago), and to pay several bills. I am also saving money for several trips to see family. (As I've mentioned, my dad had a stroke a couple years ago and I must see him.)

It is so important to me to take care of my physical needs right now, and it's been incredible to feel the abundance come in and to watch how tangible money has changed my life. I did it through listening to my spirit, not listening to the external realm.

Just as the autumn trees have many colors, there will be many external opinions all around. Tuning into your OWN color, your OWN voice is key!

This is what I do know:

- "If it is to be, it's up to me." There is nothing I can't do. I don't "need" anyone or anything. If the pure desire is there and the willingness to do *whatever* it takes to achieve it, it will happen.

Perhaps others may help us get where we are going quicker, but to adopt a belief system that says we "need" anyone or anything to be happy, productive, and on path is an illusion.

- If at any point my inner guidance steers me back to the mastermind, I will instantaneously follow the guidance. I know the money will show up to enroll again as well (if need be).
- Limiting beliefs ultimately limit us. I can choose to believe the perfect group is coming to me in perfect timing and will be affordable. Or I can choose to believe if I don't go back to this group, I'm screwed and made the "wrong" choice.
- I am able to activate the mastermind energetically all the time. The "master" mind is, literally, the combined energetic mind of those working together or focused in a direction. I can call upon any of the minds at any time, sync with that vibration, and download energy or information I may need. This, of course, is challenging for most but with practice I believe we can all tap into this energetic body for guidance. Just like we can call upon any mentor, living or deceased, to "pick their mind" for guidance. This is more along the lines of telepathy, which I believe is normal to humans who utilize the skill. I think we are shifting more in this direction as the universal consciousness grows, but that's another topic for another day!

Still with me? I went off into la-la land there for a moment.

My a-ha today was simply that regardless of what anyone might "think" or reflect to me, it is key to listen to my inner guidance. The "facts" may seem to point toward something, but if the "feeling" is not there to match it, move forward in the direction of my inner truth!

I experienced this directly today and was so overcome with emotion on my call, I began to cry — from the shear knowingness that I was *on path* and *listening* to my inner guidance. I was also emotional because I was saying out loud to this man (and myself) that I am "just so damn happy and inspired for life!" And so excited to be able to share my story with people, as well as create change on some level. It was so emotional and also so good! I love to cry sometimes out of pure emotion or knowingness. It can't be described. I have very sensitive moments, and even had them as a kid. Nature would make me cry. Or when I saw an old man eating alone in a cafe (I'm crying already.), I would cry for his heart and wish for him a partner to eat with. There were certain people I could sense a deep sadness in. Anypoo... back to the topic at hand. Emotions are a good thing! It's wonderful to let them flow.

I know I'm on path when the external is a perfect reflection of my internal feelings of goodness.

Today I ask of you – What are you lying to yourself about? What knowingness is in you that you shut out on behalf of the external voices? If it feels good, get quiet for a moment and see what answers come up regarding these questions.

Current Book – Still reading *Unbroken* by Laura Hillenbrand
Quote of the Day – "When I look back, I am so impressed again with the life-giving power of literature. If I were a young person today, trying to gain a sense of myself in the world, I would do that again by reading, just as I did when I was young." – Maya Angelou

MA OM - I AM

Day 135 – December 26, 2014

I drove "home" to the Ojai area for a very short visit during the holidays. I used to attend my friend Randee's meditation group on Monday nights. Sometimes I was the only person who would show up. Other times her small studio would be completely full and I'd take a spot on the floor (which I loved anyway). Each meditation brought new insights, stillness and often synchronicity.

Randee has what she calls her "magical" oracle deck. I believe it's Doreen Virtue's original Archangel deck. Before we go into meditation, Randee has everyone choose a card. I remember I chose the same card "manifestation" for four consecutive weeks. I keep telling Randee she better start writing her book about all of the amazing experiences related to these cards. It's truly remarkable.

The last time we gathered to meditate, we recited the "ma om" mantra. First we recited the mantra together, and then into the silence as the breath moved in and out. "Ma om" is also translated as "I am". These Indian mantras have always resonated with something deep inside me. They offer a way to connect to the breath and to bring the mind away from the chatter. Sometimes I prefer to meditate with no mantra, enjoying the sensation of my breath filling and emptying me. Other times mantras fill me up on the inhale and purify me on the exhale.

While doing the "ma om" part of our meditation, I was suddenly flashed a vision of gold walls or gold bars of some sort. They were pure solid gold and I instantly had the notion I was in Egypt in another lifetime.

I asked, "Who is here with me?"

An answer came. "Jo's here with you." (Jo is my dear friend in real life.)

I could not see Jo, but knew someone was there. I kept focusing on the gold wall in front of me and it was textured with geometric raised patterns like a map or code. I had a feeling they were DNA activation codes.

There was a moment where the vision began to fade slightly and I tried to stay with it as long as possible. It was as if I was enjoying a phenomenal dream and feeling myself wake as the dream fades away. But I was awake through this whole meditation and had the awareness of myself having the vision. I remember thinking, "Julie. This is serious. You need to remember these images."

Most of the patterns were geometric. A few organic ones were mixed in. It all became slightly blurry, but I furiously tried to jot down a couple of small impressions of what these "codes" or "keys" looked like. The photo below is from my journal. While these are not the best reproduction of what I saw, the shapes do ignite the original vision when I glance at them.

Another part of the vision was a sense of warmth. There was a glow of (perhaps) flickering flames lighting up the gold walls all around me. It was inviting. I wanted to stay. But alas, I opened my eyes, grateful for the vision of a place so remarkable. I also need to remember it's available to me anytime, anywhere. There are no boundaries. It does not "go away" or "come back".

As the ma om breathes through me, awakening the infiniteness of my soul, I smile to my heart. I smile to my breath. I smile to my vision. I smile to all those who have come before and will come after, knowing "I am" them and they are me. I am oneness.

Current Book – *Messages from Amma in the Language of the Heart* by Janine Canan
Quote of the Day – (This is the peace prayer Amma recited.)
Lokaa-ha samastaa-ha sukhino bhavantu. (three times) OM Shaanti Shaanti Shaanti-hi. *Translation:* May all beings everywhere be happy. (three times) OM. Peace to my surroundings. Peace to my heart and mind. Peace to the unseen, unknown, and unexpected.

TOP 10 REASONS TO LIVE IN A CAR

Day 141 – January 2, 2015 – 1:01 p.m.

I am *so* excited that it's 2015! 2014 was full of deep, intense emotions and massive shifts. As I gaze back at it, it's as if snow coated the old jagged cliffs and the wind blew newly formed hills into wild arrangements. While the old ones are still there, they are freshly doused with softness and a gentle rolling landscape. I would not trade last year for anything. Why do we always say this after some of the most tumultuous times of our lives? Wouldn't it be easier to say, "I would definitely trade that bad boy in for an easier year?"

This blog contains scenes from Bedwell Bayfront Park in California. Many walks and great sparks of inspiration happened here.

Somehow, after these ebbs and flows of difficult times, we have a sense that they are integral to the "becoming-ness" of our true selves. If I did not experience the depth of love, the depth of loss, and the depth of rebirth I experienced in 2014, this blog/book would likely never have been born. I also would not have known the freedom I experience day to day. Keeping this freedom in mind, I'd like to share with you some "up sides" to moving into a vehicle as a living space. I could dwell in the darkness of negatives such as the pain I feel when I have to pee at night, the careful precautions I must take in where I park to sleep, the bitter cold as I wake in the morning, etc. But these I find are just things I've learned to look at, acknowledge, and move forward to other priorities. It's not that I deny certain less-than-preferable conditions. I just don't have immediate solutions to how I live currently, so I focus on what great freedoms I've begun to know and appreciate those instead.

Simple landscapes remind me to declutter.

Here we go – these are my top ten reasons why living in a car kicks some big 'ole beautiful booty, baby!

1. No one (including the government) can keep tabs on me. At what point did we authorize people and institutions we don't know personally to keep tabs on our living spaces, our bills, our lives in general? It's a nice feeling to know that I can choose a point on planet earth and no one can find me. It's not about the desire to disappear. It's about the feeling of true freedom, knowing that the earth is everyone's space. It's not the government's space. They don't need to place a pin in me and locate me twenty-four hours a day. (Granted, my debit card keeps me visible but you catch the drift of what I'm saying.)

2. I can come and go as I please. I don't answer to roommates, curfews, family, or anyone else. I don't have to be quiet or be loud or talk when I don't want. I can get in my car or get out of my car anytime I want, anywhere I want, and answer to myself.

3. I see much more than I used to, and even hear more than I used to. When I look back on the last few months, I can see how sitting quietly in my car reading or meditating has brought me a concentrated dose of animal/nature experiences I otherwise tend not to see and also experiences of deeper audio perception. I hear sounds around me very clearly.

4. My intuition has kicked in more profoundly. While always intuitive, I've automatically become more so in needing to tune in to the people around me, the cars around me, where I park, how I park, who's watching me, if people are watching me, etc. The most important thing is staying safe and to do that I must be acutely aware of the vibrations around me. Sometimes I drive past a parking spot I stayed the previous night because it doesn't "feel" right. Nothing is different about it; I just know inside that there is a better choice. And I listen to that.

5. I save money. In a month and a half I saved $600. (In a city that costs $1500 or more for a shitty studio apartment, now you understand better why I am unable to pay rent after I pay all my bills). If I really tried hard, I could maybe find a room for

$800-1200 per month. If I spent that, I would have little to no money for food, travel, seeing family, savings, entertainment, or building my business. What a great blessing that I can now begin saving money and catching up on credit card bills.

6. I learn more. I'm reading voraciously and studying at the library constantly. 2015, I believe, is the year where I really grow my consciousness and take care of myself.

7. I wake with the sunlight. As soon as people can see into my car, I wake up. I do not want anyone knowing I am sleeping in my car, so I do my best to wake before sunrise. This provides me extra time in nature or doing what I want instead of sleeping in late at a home.

8. My level of gratitude has grown immensely. As soon as you lose virtually all comforts, you get grateful for the smallest things – peeing when you want, stretching out fully at night to avoid back and knee pain, the ability to entertain, to cook, etc.

9. Life becomes simplified. How complicated can you be when everything you need fits in a ten to twelve square foot space?

10. I've surrendered the ego (on most occasions). It is one of the most painful and simultaneously beautiful things ever to tell the people you love that you've lost everything except your heart. The people who really love you and trust you are still a success of a person step forward, and the ones who don't end up not mattering. Surrender is part of the path to spiritual enlightenment. To burn off the ego is to step into that place where the opinions of others have no bearing anymore. I've been granted this gift and now understand on a deeper level why people on spiritual journeys tend to go through so much, emotionally, in short periods of time, often many times over a lifetime.

My hope is a few of you may read this and feel less dread about your situation. Or maybe one of you had to downsize, but did it with a sad heart. Perhaps you can look at this list and see what freedoms you have been gifted and begin to shift your perspective.

Aaaaahhhh. Breathe deeply.

Everything, after all, is perspective. The naysayers will shout, "You're in denial! You're just pretending you're okay, but really your situation sucks."

Do not listen to others around you. Listen to the heart and knowingness within. The greatest, richest, most successful people in the world have all battled something deeply difficult. Many of the richest people in the world have gone bankrupt several times. They've gone from penniless to total financial freedom. Your perspective about your situation will call in the next experience you have. Are you vibrating gratitude, faith, trust, love, and appreciation for all the goodness in this moment? Expect more of it! Are you crying the blues in a wallowing soup of victimhood? Well, you'll need to shift your perspective a bit before you draw any positive experiences to you.

Pay attention to the beauty in all seasons.

As the great Earl Nightingale said, "The strangest secret is you become what you think about most of the time."

Current Book – *I Can See Clearly Now* by Wayne Dyer (One of my all-time favorite books. The number of synchronicities I experienced while reading this was incredible. It's also a very powerful book for anyone looking to step into their power along the path to their dreams.)
Quote of the day – "The most beautiful people we have known are those who have known defeat, known suffering, known struggle, known loss, and have found their way out of the depths. These persons have an appreciation, a sensitivity, and an understanding of life that fills them with compassion, gentleness, and a deep loving concern. Beautiful people do not just happen." – Wayne Dyer from the above book

AVATARS, ANGELS, AND LOVE

Day 141 – January 2, 2015 – 5:38 p.m.

I just experienced a miracle. As I was walking a path through a park in town, I saw an empty bench under a small spread of redwood trees. I instantly thought about how cold it feels outside, how glad I am not to have to sleep on that bench, and about Peace Pilgrim. I remember reading about how she would command herself to lay down and sleep, whether on a bench or the grass, regardless of the external circumstances. That is the true power of an avatar (in my opinion).

As I rounded the path a bit, a lady was sitting bundled up on it. I had full view of the whole area during the time it took me to think the above thoughts. And yet this woman appeared out of nowhere. It's nearly dark, it's cold, and she's sitting on the cold bench. Although the exact view of the bench disappeared for a few seconds, I could see the whole open area containing the path, grass, and a few trees. The lady appeared out of thin air. If she wasn't sitting on the bench when I first noticed it, she would have had to approach it from somewhere. This area was in view at all times and yet I did not see anyone approach the bench.

The world truly works in mysterious ways. It brings tears to my eyes because some great energetic force is listening (even when we forget it is). Look at how quickly an angel showed up, confirming the power of the mind and the avatar within.

5:45 p.m. - *A separate journal entry*
Over the last week, my meditations have been cleansing my emotional field. I've noticed more and more synchronicities and have been recording them (what we focus on grows). Spirit is helping me cry and release. I don't know (or even have to know) entirely what is being released. Within the release is also a filling up with the realization of the divine within everyone and everything. I get many images that flood through me, filling my body with chills.

As mentioned before in other blogs, I see my cat, Ellie, and my ex most often during these divine moments. I cannot hold either of them in my mind for a second without tearing up. It's not at all a feeling of grief or loss. It feels very sacred and beautiful. There's a deep love and sense of divine connection when feeling their energies.

At one point, due to the "wrongs" and "lies" that were done *to* me (that being the illusion, as we create everything through our own energy), I lost the ability to see/feel the truth, love, and divinity in my ex. The gift I've received on the other end is to be able to feel into the pure presence of this woman without owning the negativity, pain, or victimhood. Some masters have said the "real" work begins when we've moved out of the trauma and begin to allow for the purifying of the energy between two otherwise resistant people.

Not only is my past relationship seeming to be healed, my financial picture is turning around a bit as well. I've saved money to visit dear family I've been unable to see, which feels very abundant. As the emotional and financial healing take place, they are mirrored by the Doreen Virtue oracle readings she gifts the world with. Many of the cards have been related to prosperity and abundance during the times my money comes flowing in.

There are also cards I'm pulling about romance, beloveds, and twin flames. The theme has been about realizing a re-connection with past loves. Not that this means to re-kindle a relationship, but to re-connect from a new energy. The cards have been about the empowerment of choosing love between two people versus the opposite anger trap people tend to fall into.

Isn't it so interesting when the heart and mind know such different things? My heart knows the pure beauty of the love between myself and my ex; and my mind has total knowingness that being together would create toxicity in both of our lives. I think often times people cannot rectify the two. If only they could love one another into freedom. I posted a video about liberating love that Maya Angelou did in one of my past entries. The liberation of love allows us to feel into it and also not box it into having to be a romantic relationship. We forget to trust this and assume it's all or nothing. Either we are together and love each other or we're apart and we hate each other. Not so! We can love deeply and set free. Makes me cry to feel that. Dang. Everything makes me cry these days. It's beautiful!

I miss being held and holding. There's a part of me that can't imagine going a lifetime and not making love again to someone I was able to go so deep with. (If you have not cried the tears of divinity while making love to someone, you have not lived!) But what a gift I was given! I'll not ever settle for less than that depth. In fact, I know it will go even deeper. Some people never experience depth like this, or can never conceive of it in the first place. And of course I'm compassionate for those who won't catch a glimpse of the depth of love that is available. May they catch it in their next incarnation!

It's a challenge for my ex and me, but I treasure the friendship we've been able to step into. It's fragile like a newborn baby egg, freshly cracked. But I trust spirit will guide us into exactly where we need to be on this great spiritual journey. As my friend Randee says after our meditations, "On the deepest level, we know all is truly well."

Current Book – *I Can See Clearly Now* by Wayne Dyer
Quote of the Day – "Consequently, heading out on my own with a family to support at the age of 36, with no guaranteed income, was a monumental thing for me. I loved the idea of being my own boss, but I dreaded the thought of not being able to provide for my family and myself. What feels much clearer to me now that I look back on this risky move is the importance of feeling the fear – of acknowledging it rather than pretending it wasn't there – and then doing what my heart and soul were telling me I had to do. It was my willingness to align my body and its actions with its highest self, which could no longer handle living a lie. As I traveled the country, and then the world, doing what I knew was my Divine purpose, everything began to fall into place." – Wayne Dyer from the book above

NOISE AND INNER GUIDANCE (OR RATHER...SEEING CLEARLY)

Day 151 – January 12, 2015 – 3:47 p.m.

It's been a "noisy" few days! Holy cripes. On January 5th, a mentor I had been working with told me a story I had written for his book project would not be included. This story was to be part of a project I worked on with this gentleman and several other friends and participants, describing where I am now compared to where I was a year ago.

One would think it would devastate me not to be part of something I worked on for a year. But my first reaction was to smile. I smiled inside, knowing this story must be so special and so powerful, it's meant to live somewhere else.

Don't let anyone steal your light!

202

At the time, I had no idea this story was virtually the exact introduction I needed for this book. In a past blog, I mentioned the inner knowingness came to release my past mentor and a new one would show up who I resonated more deeply with. (Fast forward almost one year, and that person did show up.) People cling tightly to how things have to look. For example, if you begin college, you must finish college. If you make a plan to go somewhere on vacation, you must arrive only at the planned places. If you start a coaching program, you must keep going until an assumed point. We forget that the inner knowingness is more important than the logistics of what you've begun. I'm not preaching self-sabotage or giving up on your dreams. I'm talking about listening to that inner voice when it steers you away from one thing and toward another.

The most powerful lesson I learned through all of this is how to surrender. While there were some initial emotions and the desire to defend all I worked deeply on for a year, it quickly dissipated as I felt the possibilities open up. The universe is much bigger than one book, one person, or one opportunity. We are infinite beings and infinite creators. I chose to surrender to the highest good for my story. Perhaps if none of this happened, I would never have started my next book!

The new year is definitely bringing swift changes. In addition to the situation above, it's been a huge challenge at work to create harmony among extremely resistant people. I work in a retail store with people who make very little money, can't afford to live in the Bay Area, and are filled with anger. I haven't met one yet who feels they're aligned with what they really want to do in life. They also are very passive aggressive. One gentleman wrote down notes after watching me for a month, took me into the leadership office, and proceeded to nitpick every single thing I did not do perfectly during my first month. He also called me several horrifying names. The people I work with sweat all the small stuff. They are obsessed with the minutia that has no relation to running an effective team. But I am nonetheless there for a reason and I know part of it includes increasing my self-love.

Sometimes all it takes to move us out of resistance is noticing the simple beauty of a flower at dusk.

I must be honest and share with you that I was brought to tears in the meeting with my co-worker. In all the jobs I've ever worked, there has never been any personal issue with me or any resistance like I've experienced at this job (Not one person, aside from my team leader who hired me, accepted me). I communicate effectively. I love people deeply. I take on the world. I do what I can to support my team and make sure they are not overwhelmed. I'm currently doing two people's positions for the pay of one and will soon take on a third position when my team leader goes on maternity leave. No matter what I do, my team remains resistant, combative, angry, and ready to strike. But I'm proud of myself for being human, emotional, and allowing people to see the pain they can create when being cruel.

People tend to suck it all in. They think crying in the workplace will end in a lack of work (and perhaps this would be the best thing ever). But we are sentient beings. Showing the depth of feeling we have, I personally believe, is essential to both good leadership and team harmony. When my co-worker saw the level of emotion I had, he took a step back and realized just how much I took on. Since then, our work relationship has improved and I converse with him as much as I can openly.

Another opportunity arose from experiencing all the noise and resistance at work - to look within and see where some of that exists in me. After all, this job is my creation. I created myself into an angry team. I know it could definitely surface from the fact that I don't want a "job". I get angry sometimes about working for others, having to listen to other people's rules instead of my inner guidance, having to behave or speak a certain way, and much more. So my opportunity exists in releasing this resistance, or opposition to "working a job" until I make enough money through my purpose-driven projects to let the job go. And I feel that moment will arrive sooner rather than later. My dreams cannot be birthed from resistance. So I either need to quit working or find a way to align with what I do for a temporary period of time, knowing with every fiber of my being it will soon be over.

There is no accident I'm currently reading Wayne Dyer's book, *I Can See Clearly Now*. I relate to not only his writing style, but the ethical way he views business. At one point his situation mirrored mine. He was able to release his job and hit the road with his writings. I have the sense that as I publish my projects, I too can simply release the work I'm not passionate about and promote the things the universe wants me to share with the world. This book is so aligned with who I am and what I desire; it's a miracle in my life! I have a strong sense I will meet Wayne Dyer or work on a project one day. If nothing else, his work will inform mine in a very powerful way. (At the time I wrote this blog, Wayne Dyer was still living. I know I will remain connected to him through the ether forever and am so grateful for his presence in my life!)

I can see clearly that regardless of the people, resistance, or challenges that surround me, it's my choice to respond from my inner guidance. It never steers me wrong. As I look back over these last few months, I can say most people I know would ever hop into their car with a sense of adventure, knowing nothing about where their next dime would come from. But I did that, and I'm proud of myself. I created a job when I needed one. I re-connected to nature. I re-connected to my loved ones. And I'm writing my heart out, which is part of my purpose-filled mission here on this wild planet. I feel the noise settle as I think these thoughts. The truth always drowns out the noise. And the truth is that all is well and always will be.

Current book – *I Can See Clearly Now* by Wayne Dyer
Quote of the Day – "I am given a gift that is immensely beneficial. The gift is *awareness* of my secret garden – the place within me that has no restrictions, no obstacles, and where I can create for myself a way of living that is immune to any and all influences that might bring me down." – Wayne Dyer from the book above

MIRACLES ARE CHOICES

Day 153 – January 14, 2015 – 11:57 a.m.

It is not yet noon and I've already experienced three miracles, had coffee in Half Moon Bay, and did a five to six mile coast walk. I now sit at a picnic table eating a couple of bananas with my book on standby.

Yesterday I finished reading *I Can See Clearly Now* by Wayne Dyer. The experience of reading this is nothing short of miraculous. Not only did I feel a deep, other-worldly knowingness that we are soul-connected in some way, but he also sparked my mind and rekindled my lifelong fascination with the power of miracles.

This morning as I began my walk southward from Francis Beach, I was in a state of exceptional gratitude. The last time I walked this path I was gifted with a hawk experience. Birds follow me everywhere lately (as I've written about in past blogs). They come to me in magical ways and I allow myself to tune in to them more and more deeply because of this.

My morning prayer/affirmation was, "Thank you! Thank you, universe! I *know* I will experience a miracle today!"

Then I was called to thank the birds. "Thank you, birds! I love you, birds! Thank you so much!"

There was an inner sense I would experience yet another miracle with birds today. It wasn't a plea, an asking, a begging for a miracle. It was pure gratitude and exhilaration for it coming into my life with no doubt. As if it already happened (and if it didn't happen, I was so flippin' happy I wouldn't care).

If you were a bird on a path, this would be your bird's eye view!

After a few minutes a gentleman nods at me to say, "hello." I look up and to my left. A white egret is right in front of me. It's hunting. It's not off in the field, but right in front of me and allows me to come within maybe eight to ten feet of it. The egret looks at me. It then continues to hunt. It finds a rodent, keys in on it, makes a hilarious pumping gesture with its neck, and finally seizes it. I hear the rodent scream. The egret walks around, proud of its catch, shaking the rodent until it falls limp. It swoops away, then back again and proceeds to devour the rodent whole in a few gulps.

I'm stunned. How often does a person see this scene a few feet away in an open field? I say "thank you" again in my mind. I'm ecstatic with bliss and happiness to be gifted with a miracle so quickly after my prayer. So I say another prayer/affirmation of knowingness. "I *know* another miracle is coming to me today and I'm so grateful for what I've seen already."

Thanking the birds, I move down the trail, telling them they're majestic and beautiful. About ten gulls are sitting on the trail in front of me as I scan the gorgeous ocean cliffs. I whistle a friendly tune and tell them they're very special. One by one they lift off, eyeing me as I get a close glimpse. The gulls do not fly away. They circle over my head and one of them lifts off, flies directly to my left side, hovers about chest high, and stares at me as it flaps its wings.

One of several gulls that flew right past me and made eye contact. I LOVE nature!

I snap photos, knowing I can use this story to inspire people in my writing. Each gull does this as I move forward and again I am in a state of overwhelming gratitude. I'm surprised and not surprised all in one. These things are supposed to happen and are natural occurrences when we are in tune with our souls. We're taught miracles are only "really big" and "rare". I can feel in my soul that I've created miracles through my own pure energy and the intentions of gratitude and faith. As I pass the trail of gulls, the rest of my walk is filled with beauty and a tranquil feeling inside. I still have a sneaking suspicion the birds are not done joining me today. More thanks. More happiness. More feeling into my next miracle.

I forget the name, but a local type of field finch sits on the trail right next to my right foot. It's so close and still, I wonder if it's hurt. I say hello and honor its beauty. The bird tilts its head at me, slowly hops away, looks back at me, and flies away.

A few of the group still standing on the trail. Each one lifted off and looped over to me as this one did on the left.

I'm suddenly overcome with emotion regarding these three blessings I've enjoyed. I say a short prayer in my mind. "I'm so grateful for the birds and these miracles. Thank you. I know I'm soul-connected to Wayne Dyer. I know I'm supposed to learn more about miracles and to do this work in my life. I'm continuing to grow, and I'm beginning to understand."

As I release this prayer, another finch sits to the right of my foot again, barely visible in the grass. It looks at me, just like the last one and it hops so slowly I again wonder if it's hurt. We engage and it slowly hops away. Tears well up in my eyes. I know this is a direct confirmation of my prayer I just released. I say directly to the universe, "Thank you. I feel so aligned with my path."

More tears come. I'm filled with incredible peace.

My walk has come to an end. Bird miracles are only the beginning lately.

Several days ago I watched a seemingly poor Hispanic man walking past someone's porch. The man on the porch was trying to ask the guy if he needed a bike. Apparently this guy walks past the porch every day on the way to work. The gentleman only understood Spanish and couldn't understand what the bike owner was saying. He started to walk away. I leaned over the porch and asked the bike owner if I can translate with some "Spanglish". He was very happy to let me try so I yelled over to the gentleman who was walking away. After several minutes, I got him to understand that he was the new owner of a bike. I don't know how to speak Spanish. But I tried. And that's where the miracles happen. The miracle was watching that guy's face light up. He was obviously poor and had to walk to work carrying much of what he owns. There is no greater miracle than seeing someone smile or watching relief come over someone's face.

Since moving north I've been gifted with several miraculous opportunities to be of service. Not only in the instance with the gentleman above, but a few days ago I found someone's wallet next to my tire at the gym. It was the crack of dawn, still dark out, and someone would surely steal it by daylight. I gave the wallet to the gal at the gym desk and she seemed unimpressed that anyone would care about a lost wallet. This wallet was full of cash and I wasn't totally sure the desk attendant would call the guy, but let's hope. I said a prayer that the man receives his wallet in full and to have a renewed sense of the human heart, passing it forward to someone else one day.

Minutes later I found a lucky penny in front of my feet in the women's restroom stall. Maybe not the cleanest of places to be gifted with a penny (ha), but still appreciated.

We all have opportunities to create miracles in our lives. For me, it's just a level of consciousness. It's a choice. Do I want to go for a walk? Or do I want to go for a walk, filled with the knowingness that the miracle of nature is all around me? Do I want to ignore the guy who could have a nice new bike? Or do I want to try to help, thus receiving the miraculous blessing of a smile? I don't always make the choice to align with the miracles, but I'm getting better all the time.

Current Book – *Traveler's Tales: The Road Within – True Stories of Transformation* by Sean and James O'Reilly
Quote of the Day – "Whenever someone tells me about a great spot that I must check out I say, 'I'll have to put that on my list.' I just know

that no matter where I go in the world, traveling renews my faith in humankind, as well as in myself. It's a journey of remembrance back to my original self, the one who is wholly connected to all beings and nature. It's a journey that rediscovers what's really important, ultimately." – Barbara Sansone from her work "Under the Mango Tree" featured in the travel book listed above

PRESENCE IS A PRESENT

Day 171 – February 1, 2015 – 8:40 a.m.

I just finished a nice loop walk at Bedwell Bayfront Park along the marsh. The sun peeked over the hills, illuminating the trees from behind. A stunning sense of peace washed over me as I took in the grace of shifting light.

Good Morning, sunshine! Oooohhhhhhmmmmmmm...

As I came around one bend, an entire flock of small whitish colored birds flew from my right side, over my head and off to the left of me. I heard them before I saw them. It was not their chirps I heard. A buzzing vibrato, like nothing I'd heard before, washed its way through me. I am unable to describe it entirely; it was an other-worldly sound and feeling. It was as if I stepped outside myself for a moment, noticed this new sound, and watched it come closer. Then the sound/vibration moved away and I felt like I snapped back into my conscious self, wondering what the heck just happened.

Perhaps this was a moment of true presence? The observer was not "observing" but rather the "beingness" of me was just experiencing fully. I can look back now and observe, but when I was in it, there was no sense of being able to observe. The clarity of the pure experience was just happening. (In fact, I was so present I did not take any bird photos. So I'll pepper this blog with bird and nature photos from my photo vault for you.)

I've been walking the beaches and trails of California for the last eight years. Swarms of birds have flown over me of all types. This was the wildest, most kinetic thing I've heard and felt while experiencing birds. What a gift! Because I have walked, hiked, and meandered my way through extremely profound nature experiences, I often forget there's always more to expand on. Nature is infinite.

Being in nature brings me back to a level of simplicity, coupled with a sense of expansion. I come out of the dualities of "yes" and "no". I transcend my brain chatter. It's as if I feel empty and full all at once and in this balanced place, all sorts of "expanded" realities begin to happen. Call them presents, if you like. The presence brings me presents. Today's present was experiencing the pure sentient and aural vibration of birds, as if time stood still and I stepped away from the identity of human Julie. I suppose we could also call this present "oneness". The birds were not separate from me. I was not talking to them as a separate entity. I became them, sharing in what they must feel as they vibrate their flight through space.

These are American Coots. Random factoid – their feet are very colorful!

As I write, sharing with you, my sense of purpose in this world deepens. I know someone reading this will be ignited with a desire to experience nature in a pure, present way. I know someone reading this will feel something become clearer that used to be murky. I know someone reading will go for a hike tomorrow instead of turning on the television. Part of why I'm here is to help people connect to nature with a sense of awe, freedom, and expansion. I love to share what I experience; I love watching each "share" spark a flame into existence and expand the energy of goodness all through this world!

I'd love to hear about one of your purest nature experiences. Anytime we share our collective nature experiences, the desire to experience more keeps growing. Let's gift one another with presents of presence!

I wake up almost every morning to sunrises like these!

Current Book – *Traveler's Tales: The Road Within – True Stories of Transformation* by Sean and James O'Reilly
Quote of the Day – "The simplification of life is one of the steps to inner peace. A persistent simplification will create an inner and outer well-being that places harmony in one's life." – Peace Pilgrim

GIFTS BESTOWED UPON A WANDERER

Day 189 - February 19, 2015 - 7:11 a.m.

Life without a traditional home provides some incredible experiential gifts. Because I don't leave work, head home, and distract myself with various things, I am present to an enormous amount of events in my environment. I also don't hit the "snooze" button a million times before work, as my body wakes naturally with the sun as it flows through my car window. Waking early provides opportunities to capture special moments (I've included several photos here of moments I treasure.).

This morning, just after dawn, I walked onto some rocky cliffs in the Pescadero area. As I approached the edge, I saw a seal pup looking back at me from the next set of rocks. It was obviously scared and made sweet little movements with its head. The seal was likely stranded the night before as the tide receded and now it tried to find a way down the cliff.

I sat down on my cliff, singing and whistling to the pup, trying to figure out what to do. Should I call the seal rescue folks? Should I walk down the steep ledge and climb to the pup's perch? Should I leave it there for hours, hoping the high tide will provide rescue? I decided to let go, ask the universe and wait for a hunch.

A few minutes later I stood up, hiked down the cliff and headed toward the seal pup. As soon as I moved closer, the seal began to move and slid its way down to the tide. Perhaps all it needed was a little boost to get going. Perhaps it didn't live and was caught by a shark. These circumstances often make us second guess ourselves. In most cases, it's best to leave a seal pup where it is. But I had the sense the mother was near and it just needed to get to the water to find her. I asked. I listened. I acted.

I'm grateful life has gifted me with moments like these as a result of being out and about perpetually. Normally, I'd be sleeping in, putzing around the house, making breakfast, and doing a number of other normal morning duties. But now I wake before sunrise on most days and head somewhere beautiful. That, in itself, is the gift of being a wanderer/pilgrim/traveler of sorts. How many people wake up and get to watch a seal pup figure its way back to sea?

I often gaze into the eyes of the ocean each morning and ask, "Where is everyone?"

Of all the miles of coastline between Half Moon Bay and Davenport, it's extremely rare to find anyone walking the beach or even observing the sunrise. Droves of people show up to drink beer, fish, and blast their radios when the heat hits. But in general, I have about thirty to forty-five miles of coastline to myself on most mornings. That's incredible to actually quantify. There are *millions* of people who live within "doable" distance to a beach walk. Yet no one arrives. I sit, observing the waves, the pelicans, the sky colors, and beds of kelp crashing to shore. I consider that *millions* of people could do the same. But they do not.

Then I ask myself, "Julie. When you had a home, did you take advantage of the scenery accessible to you?"

These questions come up as a system of checks and balances. When I notice or point out that people are not doing something incredible they could be doing (after constantly hearing people's excuses for not getting into nature), it's healthy to check my own actions. I never want to preach about something I'm not doing myself, or at least in forward movement to it.

Yes, I did take advantage of the scenery when I had a home. I remember waking at four in the morning to beat the heat up Camelback Mountain in Phoenix years ago. I remember visiting Tasmania and as my then-partner slept in for hours, I photographed the coast. I'm not talking about the need to be out there every single day. I'm just posing the possibility that we have busied and fatigued ourselves to the point of no longer appreciating the smallest of gifts outside our front doors.

There will always be a day that sleeping in, cuddling up, and reading a good book is perfect. Or spending a day catching old movie reruns. There will also be a day the alarm gets smacked into its next mission so we can enjoy a few more moments of shut-eye. However, when we find ourselves too tired, too busy, or too uninspired to seek out the beautiful gifts and treasures all around us, it's time to re-evaluate. This is one of the gifts I've come to know, as a result of life on the road. One could say I have a thirty square mile piece of land I've been gifted with. Not too shabby for a home (less) gal, eh?

Close your eyes for a moment and dream into the beauty you can find outside your door. Perhaps today is the perfect day to enjoy these gifts!

Current Book - *The Portable Pilgrim: Seven Steps to Spiritual Enlightenment* by Susanna McMahon
Quote of the Day - "Not all those who wander are lost." - J.R.R. Tolkien

GOAT BIRTHS FOR MY BIRTH-DAY

Day 190 – February 20, 2015 – 11:26 a.m.

Yesterday was one of the most incredible days of my life! Although today is my birthday, I feel my gifts arrived a day early! It all began with the gift of meeting a seal pup, as you recently read about. Then I headed inland to one of my favorite places to visit – Harley Farms Goat Dairy. While I have mixed feelings about dairies in general (that's another conversation for another day), I've found this to be a fantastic place to connect with the goats, who are very well cared for.

Look at this furry little bundle of goodness! My heart melts.

Yesterday was also the Chinese New Year, the year of the goat! Because it's been so warm here in California, the goats were birthing a bit early. I had a feeling I would see a birth yesterday if I headed over to the farm and 'voila'; my expectations were realized.

Upon arrival, a bunch of goat kids were penned up and cuddling. They could not have been more than a few days to a week old. A mama was birthing in the barn and I was unable to see much. While everyone else stood and watched that event, I sauntered off to pet some pregnant goats who looked ready to burst. One of them began to lose some water and I knew a baby was on its way!

Mama goats cuddling.

Quantifying my excitement in words is difficult. I am profoundly connected to the animal realm. My friends are always crapping their pants when wild animals or farm animals come to me out of nowhere. (My cousin calls me Dr. Doolittle and asks me what animals I will be summoning from the ether during each visit.) I pet a wild pelican on a pier once and cows often let me scratch them on the side of the road. That's just the beginning. So if you can imagine how that translates to a goat farm – oh my gosh, it was heavenly!

The goat whose water burst came over to me along the fence. She looked up at me and then kept popping up and sitting down, using her hooves to create a nest environment in the earth. She panted and had some light contractions. I petted her sides and sweet face, scratched her hips, and told her she's doing well. Over and over I told her, "You're doing good, Mama. You're going to have a beautiful baby!"

Mama nestled up at my feet on the other side of the fence. I wished we were on the same side. She breathed heavier, made adorable sounds, and suddenly bigger contractions came. After a few minutes I saw the embryonic sac push its way out. Bits of white and black fur were visible in the sac. I filmed for about ten minutes at which point my camera yelled at me that there was no time left on the chip. At that point, most of the head was out, but still inside the sac. Talk about an incredible sight to behold! I had never seen a live birth before, so my heart was pounding like crazy. I tried not to alert the crowd so I could enjoy this quiet moment with Mama goat.

If you look closely, you can see the very first part of the sac here.

It was so beautiful to see the sac, like a small balloon full of red veins that nourished the babe on its way out. Mama curled around and around, prepping her udders. She stood up, using gravity as a helper as she moved closer to me. I had the deepest sense of connection with this goat. From the moment she first let me pet her swollen sides to this moment of direct communication, I knew we were experiencing something very special together. At one point, just before the baby came, Mama looked into my eyes and said some goat words. It was a moment beyond description.

I spoke to her softly again and encouraged peace for this birth. She spun around and the whole kid suddenly fell out of her in one big plop. She had moved away a little with the advance of all the people who came running to watch the birth (funny how humans seem to ruin a quiet and special moment with their noise).

Another goat mama, still pregnant, came to claim the newborn. (I had no idea goats try to steal each others' babies.) The two mamas licked the sac open. The head was still covered and I could see the sac bubble with each breath in and out. The baby goat cried and Mama licked it continuously. It was finally freed from the sac and it stood up immediately, wobbling and falling a few times.

Little angel-face was just born. I was a sappy mess! This was a few minutes after Mama cleaned him up.

The pregnant goat started getting dominant, trying to steal the baby again. I grabbed the other goat so the baby could find its mother's nipple and begin to nurse, which was the most amazing and beautiful sight. I watched mother and kid bond for the next hour or two. That morning I had read about being on purpose, or aligned with our souls. Time is no longer linear and we feel we've entered a time warp. This was exactly what I was experiencing. A total of four hours on this goat farm felt like fifteen minutes.

After the crowd subsided, I continued talking to Mama and told her how beautiful her baby was. It was truly stunning, all black with a white face like a cow. His tail was also white. If I had a house, I would have taken that goat home. No questions asked. Mama then brought her baby over to me along the fence and leaned her chin up for a scratch. I cuddled her over the fence, praising her for being such a strong lady. I reached my hand through the fence near the ground and scratched the kid's body, now slightly dry and full of soft sunlit tufts of fur. I held its little head in my hand. Mama bent her head down and told me she was proud and was approving of me touching her baby.

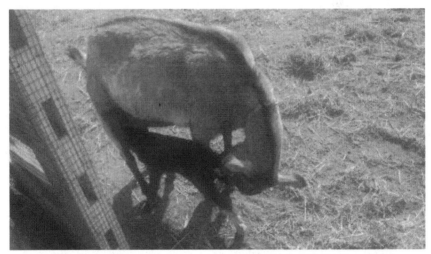

First sip of milk! Baby goats are so alert right after birth. Incredible!

The whole pen was empty. The other goats had been moved to the pasture after their births and Mama had come over to me to share the beauty she created. I will be grateful for and treasure that goat for a lifetime. I think that goat knew and felt my reverence for her. I could watch baby goats every day and never get bored. A true birthday gift, for sure!

This is the point when Mama brought her baby to meet me. I'll treasure this beautiful moment forever!

I ended the day back on the coast at low tide, playing in tide pools and climbing up rocks covered in pelican poop (good times). A little boy was screaming out, "Look Dad! Sea enemies! Sea enemies are everywhere!" (He used this word instead of "anemones".)

Then he said to himself, "Actually, you guys are sea *friends*, not enemies." His face was completely serious and adorable in every way.

Thus, the day before my birthday was full of treasures I'll hold in my heart forever, including the reminder that our "enemies" are actually our friends!

To view my brief video of the newborn goat, visit the link below!

https://www.youtube.com/watch?v=AIqgXu4dHJE

Current book – *The Portable Pilgrim: Seven Steps to Spiritual Enlightenment* by Susanna McMahon

Quote of the Day – "From sunrise to sunset, I was in the forest, sometimes far from the house, with my goat who watched me as a mother does a child. All the animals in the forest became my friends, even dangerous and poisonous ones. Thanks to my goat-mother and my Indian nurse, I have always enjoyed the trust of animals—a precious gift. I still love animals infinitely more than human beings." – Diego Rivera

WHAT DO *YOU* WANT?

Day 196 – February 26, 2015 – 6:33 p.m.

Every blog could easily begin with the words, "What an incredible day!"

The face of love.

Today I went back to the goat farm and also visited the elephant seals at Año Nuevo State Park. The day was so good; I felt like I was in a dream! Elephant seals sprawled out along the beach, scratching their bellies in between bouts of sleep. Most of the females were at sea feasting after a long month or two of giving their milk to the babies. Soon the babies would be learning to swim and feed at sea. The males continue to fight and claim their mighty harem of females. One male often mates with and protects fifty females. Can you imagine? Cripes! I guess "keep it simple" is the best policy, as we surely can't hold down more than a couple mates at a time before mayhem happens. So much to consider and learn from a bunch of elephant seals sunbathing, eh?

Well hello there! A little wave from Sir Elephant Seal.

When I arrived at the goat farm, the owner was shifting a few of the week old goats around so they would have more space in a larger pen. She asked me to do her a favor and pass one of the goat kids off to someone behind the barn. Doing *her* a favor? More like doing *me* a favor! I had never held a baby goat in my arms. As she handed me the goat, it smelled of fresh goat milk and it nestled its nose into my hair, trying to milk my neck. Ha! The amount of love I had for that little soul was off the charts. The goat was much mellower than I would have imagined. Typically baby animals are fussy and hyper. This little one flopped around in my arms like it was lounging poolside waiting for a goat milk colada.

During the last few months, traveling around on this wild adventure, I notice many "words" or "conditionings" I experienced while young, come back to me. They usually pop into my mind during quiet moments. Various people throughout my life have said similar things to me such as, "You don't want to live in such a small town." Or, "You're too young to be living so far out from a big city. You're young and should be where the activity is!"

This is the beautiful goat kid I wrote about in the last blog. He's only 7 days old here and growing fast!

Feet + Seaweed = Happiness

At the time, these things seemed normal to hear. In fact, I almost believed the people around me. I'd catch myself thinking things like, "Maybe I should move to a big city and then I'll be able to 'meet people' and 'be happy' and 'do fun activities'."

But wait a minute! I always meet people, my life is full of happiness, and I do all sorts of activities. I'm a perpetual traveler right now, so I probably do more activities than most city folks. Maybe I don't go to as many bars or restaurants, but I'm exposed to a huge variety of cultures and experiences lately.

I *want* the kind of lifestyle where I have a large piece of gorgeous land to grow my veggies. A place where I can hop on my bike and enjoy the waves a short ride away, visit the seals, pick shells, and breathe in rhythm with the waves. I want salty air, green hills, smiling earthy people, and space to frolic to and fro!

People mean well when they say, "you're this" or "you want that". Perhaps we can check in and see if we're telling anyone we love what they want in life. Maybe we should begin asking people what they want, what they dream of, what's beating through their hearts!

Yes, I love big cities. Yes, I love the hustle and bustle of great restaurants, a night of dancing, the wind whipping through tall Chicago buildings, and watching streams of people in all their individual glory.

But when I come home, I like the cool earth beneath my feet, grasshoppers chirping, the stars above me sparkling into infinity, intimate gatherings with dear loved ones, the soft glow of a fireplace, making sweet love with no one around to hear our sacred cries of ecstasy and most of all – the pure peace and quiet gift of nature.

Sometimes simplicity takes my breath away.

What do **you** want? What would make your heart sing the song of a morning finch?

Current Book – *Buddha* by Deepak Chopra
Quote of the Day – "How can freedom be taught except by someone who is free?" – Deepak Chopra from the book above

IN THE FLOW

Day 202 – March 4, 2015 – 6:58 p.m.

After six days straight and several 4-5:00 a.m. shifts, I'm off work today and tomorrow. I'm feeling a bit pooped. I drove out to the coast tonight for a mighty gorgeous beach walk along the pier area of Half Moon Bay. The evening was crystal clear. Tomorrow I will likely hike at Butano State Park!

Here's a preview... I did hike at Butano State Park and will share more in my next blog!

This week my gut instinct was confirmed when my boss at work told me she will be moving back east with her family. This means I could apply for her position (I'm currently doing her position as well as mine since she's been on maternity leave.). I was hired externally by the company I work for. (My company claims they almost never do that for leadership positions as they prefer to hire internally, so people are familiar with their "culture".) Just three and a half months after starting the position, I may apply for an even higher leadership position should I choose to. When I am "in the flow" and loving life, opportunities arrive out of nowhere. This doesn't mean I'll get the position, or even desire applying for it, but the option to apply, in itself, brings a feeling of abundance.

Another gift appears!

There's often a missing link for people when they attempt to find a job, or bring in new/better opportunities. They furiously "look" for things outside themselves, as I wrote about in my introduction. They forget that the attraction of what they desire floats on a wave of vibration. I currently feel empowered because I've taken on three positions at once, am raising sales, and doing some other incredible stuff at work. Therefore, an opportunity came to me without even looking for it. I can't say I completely resonate with the company or people I work for, but the option to apply for something is empowering in itself. This feeling of empowerment is bringing me more experiences of having more empowering choices.

The most important thing right now is to focus on my side projects, my writing, and all that makes my heart sing. I'm not the usual employee at work. People are always looking to "move up" and I'm looking to "move out". It's a bill payer for a brief period of time until I make enough money off my passions to no longer need it.

Came across this bounty of miners lettuce on one of my "in the flow" walks. I sat down and grazed like a farm animal. These tender succulent leaves are full of water. My favorite wild green!

I'm loving this feeling of being "in the flow" of life and watching the universe answer my calls of bliss with new experiences that feel blissful. I am able to be of service at work, helping the public increase their level of health. This makes my heart smile. Then I leave work and I get to see some of the most dramatic and beautiful coastal areas in the country. People come from all over the world to experience what I get to experience virtually daily. These things outside work keep me balanced and in the correct vibration to bring in more of the same.

Two days ago, in another moment of total tranquil flow, a bird came to me. The bird flew out of nowhere, landed on the hood of my car and proceeded to interact with me. It stood on the windshield, then hopped down, then hopped back up to the hood, looked inside the car, peeped a little, hopped back down, and eventually landed on my left side mirror. It stared at me, chirped a little, and left.

This is when the bird first arrived. It looked straight at me and began to sing its sweet little bird song.

Just after the bird jumped off my windshield to the ground and back up to the mirror to chat.

The more "in the flow" I feel, the more I experience gifts such as this bird joining me in conversation. Opportunities, gifts, great conversations, and all sorts of wonders arrive when I live this sort of surrendered life. It's difficult to put into words, but essentially I'm aligned with all that feels good. That alignment brings great waves of more places, people, events, opportunities, experiences, and feelings that resonate with who I really am. This is what I love to share with others.

I can't wait to share this with people. I can't wait to show people how they can live their dreams, even if they don't have every single physical thing they want yet. I can't wait to help people get into vibrational alignment, so they too can live from within! Now that flow feels fabulous!

Current Book – *Buddha* by Deepak Chopra
Quote of the Day – "Learn to use your memories... Don't let them use you." – Deepak Chopra from the book above.

MEDITATING WITH BANANA SLUGS

Day 203 - March 5, 2015

A cool, mist-covered morning blossomed into a sun-drenched hike along quiet streams at Butano State Park. No one was on the trail except me until the last hour of my hike. The wet smell of leaves, redwood bark, and wild herbs clouded my mind with a haze of anticipation. I get giddy with excitement as I approach a quiet trail. Just as someone salivating for a chocolate chip cookie as the buttery

243

goodness hits their nostrils, I too salivate for the wildness of sensations that come so easily in nature. My dad always taught me about nature. He would say in a kid voice, "Hello grandfather tree. Oh, I love you." And he would proceed to hug that tree. I have many memories of tree hugs and plunging our noses into the bark of certain pine trees (which smell of vanilla perfume).

Hello grandfather tree!

Nature, I believe, really awakens our humanness. Humans are sentient. Some of us dull our senses or even fear senses we are naturally created to experience. I know people who would be scared to smell into the puzzle-piece bark of a ponderosa pine. They think a spider would crawl into their noses and lay eggs. I know people who think dirt is stinky. These people have never smelled dirt birthed of leaves, twigs, insects, and dew. The only dirt they've experienced is the sludge and runoff from factory farms - a putrid mixture of bacteria, feces, urine, and God-only-knows-what. I feel so blessed to know what dirt is and not need any therapy sessions to work through any "fears" of the natural environment.

What I learned from my dad is something so profound and powerful; I can't begin to encourage you enough to get your kids into the dirt, into nature in all its glorious forms. As a direct sentient result of my time in nature, I confidently hiked alone beginning at the age of thirteen all over Phoenix, Arizona. Part of why I exist is to help people release their irrational fears of nature (or even their disconnection from it) and step into beautiful, authentic experiences of presence in natural environments.

These memories and thoughts come to me as I walk slowly through the towering trees. The redwoods breathe deeply as the fog settles upon their tiny leaflets. I look up, excited to teach my incredible little nephew about the animals and trees of this area. I even made him a video about owls, filming various parts of this trail. He lives in Florida and video is often a tool I use to share with his beautiful soul. Thoughts come, thoughts go. I walk. More thoughts come. More people arrive in my mind's eye. Then they go. I walk.

A little yellow speck catches my eye. The speck becomes bigger as I turn toward it. It almost startles me. I notice how unfamiliar things startle me as I take them in for the first time. It seems I've encountered a banana slug (I'd only heard about them a few times.).

I stare at it, entirely consumed for several minutes. It does move. Barely. I see an opening on the side. I'm unsure if these are breathing holes or some other type of orifice. I stare some more. It's so bright and beautiful. What a wonder of the world! Is it wondering about me as well? I take my time watching the slug's movements, not realizing I'd be seeing many more.

I find these slugs to be so beautiful.

A stream crossing appears. I sit to meditate, gazing briefly at the stream and surroundings. Sorrels poke their heads up all around me, sheltered by mushrooms. A huge spider web sits over the creek, hanging from a tree. The sounds of gentle, running water rush through my veins, cleansing me. I'm grateful. I'm at peace. I long to live along streams like these and near oceans like the one just a few miles away. The air is still, but alive with the redwoods speaking to one another. They are a community, holding hands high above me. Their shelter warms my heart. I see the lifeforce all around me pushing its way through my veins, just as the creek pushes its way up the limbs of each tree. They're symbiotic and I notice my own symbiosis with the environment. I forget this too often. Everywhere I go (not just on the trail) I am in constant exchange with my environment. This leads me to the reminder to be very cautious of my environment, to surround myself with the lightest of energies.

After a short while I stand and proceed to walk. More banana slugs appear. They cling to branches at eye height. I look deeply into them. I see every single bump and ridge along their slinky-like bodies. One of them sticks its eyes out, staring back at me in curiosity. We carry on for a while, knowing each other on some level.

Later a newt crosses my path. This is my first experience with a newt, as well. I had seen "Slow down! Newt crossing!" signs earlier. People say sightings are rare. A little goose-bumped newt made its way to the running water slowly, hand over foot (or maybe foot over foot). I watched its instinct, so beautifully set within its biology, guide him/her back to the moist environment over each twig and leaf. Its little feet reminded me of a child's tiny delicate hands, fresh from the womb. Then I consider how incredible the newt's soft feet are to carry it over such rough terrain. It must have a resilient heart. Again, I consider things that come to me, passing through me like waves of insights or memories. I consider the children's book I wrote and never published. While the main character is a gecko, its feet carry it over a very rough terrain and I am now witnessing what my heart poured forth years ago. I will publish this book. I will read to children and adults. I will remind them of the resilience of the heart.

Please visit the link below for a video of the newt.

https://www.youtube.com/watch?v=Umqr_57f24M

My heart is full.

Two banana slugs sit to the left of the trail. They are *drenched* in slime. This slime, I eventually learned, keeps them moist and also contains pheromones for attracting a mate. The two slugs in the photo and video below are obviously deeply in love. They are also hermaphrodites. I consider my own sliding scale of gender expression, often not feeling entirely female yet completely embracing my femaleness. My hair grows long. Then it's short. I dance on the beach in a sundress. Then I feel studly in a suit and tie at a drag party. It all doesn't matter a whole lot to me. It's just simply the present expression of what's flowing through me. Like the Kinsey scale of sexuality (straight to homosexual), we all fit somewhere on the scale of masculine to feminine, and everything in between. These slugs remind me of the containment of both expressions within us. How beautiful.

Banana slug love, baby!

It's also beautiful how these two make love to each other. It's slow and meticulous and attentive. One could even say it's "sensual". Oh, horrors! Did I just call banana slugs "sensuous"?

Yes. Yes I did. We can see all expressions of life in nature if we're present and open to it. (Visit the video below and feel the love!)

https://www.youtube.com/watch?v=wFweclu3TIU

My heart is full.

I feel my heart beating slightly fast with amazement for what I'm capturing on camera. I also watch without the camera, to be fully present to it. I know the camera is my tool to share with others and awaken new feelings/thoughts within them, but I enjoy the experience of turning it all off as well.

My heart is full.

Mushroom friend pushing its way through the earth.

I long for my dad to be with me. I wrote in a previous blog that he had a stroke several years ago. He's only about sixty-four right now. He went from doing one hundred mile bike marathons to losing the use of his right side. His depression comes and goes. He has a young second family to care for. He lives far from me. But somewhere within, I *know* a great miracle is coming to him. I *know* he will be on trails with me again one day, regardless of how slow we must walk. I *know* he will teach others what he taught me about the smell of nature and being totally present to this incredible gift of being human. If you have a moment or two to send him some good vibrations from your heart, I would be so grateful. I posted a photo below so you can have something to focus on. His name is Elliot and he's a great man.

My heart is full.

Please enjoy these few seconds of a water meditation I captured for you. A small slice of the heaven I experienced today. You can visit the link below.

https://www.youtube.com/watch?v=qfVP9WflYOs

Here's my dad! Always happy in nature. Please envision him on the trails!

Current Book - *Buddha* by Deepak Chopra
Quote of the day - "The most beautiful thing we can experience is the mysterious; it is the source of all true art and science."- Albert Einstein

BOOKS ARE MAGNETIC

Day 234 – April 5, 2015

Do you ever experience a book landing in your life *exactly* when you need it? And if so, do you acknowledge the miracle-of-sorts that occurs? "Miracle" tends to be a big buzz word these days. I'm not talking about a phantom event in which we have no part in the creation of something - and I also don't mean we should pretend a big fluffy "light being" passes out books like candy to kids. This is more of a co-creation happening in which you are moving along, noticing feelings and desires, and suddenly the books show up, meeting those feelings and thoughts you disperse over a period of time.

Like beams of light, I send out feelings to the world which guide me to books that meet my inner most desires.

252

This happens more and more frequently. The more I acknowledge it, the more it happens. I call myself an "amazing book manifestor", not only because I love books and want to throw lots of appreciation and energy toward them, but also because I seem to find the perfect book in perfect timing!

Since moving into my truck I've had a knowingness that my next book I'm writing is in the works. Although not the ideal living situation, it has inspired more writing than I've done in the last five years. The blog you're reading now is part of my next book. (That sentence was written before this book was published and here we are!)

It's a strange experience to write a book and look back on it. Suddenly, what was of utmost importance a few months ago is no longer relevant. It makes me question whether I should bother publishing something that no longer relates to my current life. But we must not forget that the messages arriving months ago might be the perfect thing for someone who needs to hear it in the present. It doesn't matter if we grow and find past writings to be ghosts of our past selves. The most important thing, in my opinion, is to remember that ideas come through us to serve a purpose. It's not always about our own lives. It's about someone else, how that idea or message can serve someone, whether now or in a thousand years. Our writing begins to take on a life of its own. My job is to give it life. Then set it free and hope it lands on someone's soul to create a spark of light.

I have lucid visions of speaking and writing, as if already created. Thus I attract more and more stories about people who have done the same. Wayne Dyer's *I Can See Clearly Now* came to me recently, as I mentioned earlier. It's a virtual play-by-play account of how he ditched his job he no longer wanted, trusted himself and the universe, and embarked on a journey in which he shared his book with the world. He visited radio shows, book stores, and anyone else who would give him a platform to share about his book. And as a result, he became hugely successful.

What stuck out most about Dr. Dyer's story is his total sense of trust when embarking on his journey. While the world around him clearly thought he was nuts for leaving a fantastic university position with many perks, he knew he had a different mission. There was no option anymore. I, too, feel that moment coming very soon for me. I know I must share my gifts with the world. I know my next book will inspire masses of people. I know my story parallels Wayne Dyer's in too many ways to count. Reading his book was like talking to my best friend at a coffee shop, hugely engrossed in our conversation.

It seems almost every book I come in contact with these days is magnetic. A book called *The Story of my Heart* was shining with beams of light (no exaggeration) in the middle of the Half Moon Bay Library shelf. It was an old book by Richard Jefferies in which he shares his love of nature and feelings of ecstatic bliss. My experiences in nature I last wrote about brought me similar feelings (actually, nature always does this for me) and thus reading his book was, again, like reading the story of my own current heart/mind. I find it so interesting that the books I need magnetize themselves into my life in divine moments. This book could have come to me while I sat depressed, watching television for months. It came exactly when I resonated with its message – as I traveled the trails and felt the waves of supreme bliss overtake my conscious mind.

Due to my pilgrim-like lifestyle, I have been thinking a lot about hiking "El Camino de Santiago" in Spain. I've been drawn to these types of walks my whole life. Thus, I magnetized to Shirley MacLaine's book *The Camino*. My heart also felt a synergy with her as I read, knowing I will be there one day learning and growing into deeper parts of my soul.

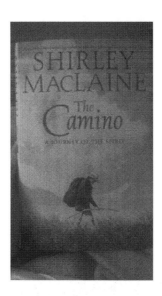

I suppose this blog is nothing more than gratitude for the magnetic way books show up and a reminder to all of us to notice the synchronicities, however small they may be.

As the world plugs into their computers, games, and tablets, my heart comes home to the sweet sound of pages turning, the subtle mass of textured print, and the many smells each book holds as I pass through it.

May you magnetize effortlessly to the next book that will radically change your life!

Current Book - *The Story of my Heart* by Richard Jefferies and *The Camino* by Shirely MacLaine
Quote of the Day - "The more I traveled the more I realized that fear makes strangers out of people who should be friends." - Shirley MacLaine

RESPONSIBILITY VERSUS BLAME

Day 268 - May 9, 2015

The words "I'm to blame" conjure up feelings of guilt, shame, powerlessness, and defeat. "Blame" is associated with "fault". We're often taught, at a very young age, that when something is someone's fault, this person was obviously intentionally doing something wrong or bad. We hear phrases like, "Don't blame me," or "It's not my fault." This sense of blaming people does not usually result in growth or empowerment - due to its negative connotation. People would rather hide in a corner than be "to blame" for something.

Who, me? I didn't do it. I'm just chillin' with m'cantaloupe.

There is, however, an empowered way to acknowledge wrong-doing. (I hesitate to use the term "wrong-doing" as even the mistakes we make are harmoniously entwined for our ultimate growth and "right-doing".) We could change this term to "less than preferable events" for the purposes of this blog. Hopefully you catch my drift. Essentially, you make a choice, a result happens, and it's often less-than-preferable.

Two things might happen. You might ignore/deny it or you might acknowledge/take responsibility for it.

A mentor of mine said "taking 100% responsibility" for *everything* in your life is a five second miracle. Yes, *everything*!

Okay, you guys. I take full responsibility for drinking all the milk and then slamming my feet on the bucket until someone brings me more. I'll be more patient next time.

I can hear some of your thoughts. "Screw you! I didn't create my flu! It's not my fault my store was robbed. Being homeless was not my choice. My metabolism is off; I can't help it if I gain weight."

These are disempowered thoughts. These thoughts are the ones that surface when you fear you are "to blame" for something. This blame feels like deep shame within every cell you have. There's no room for blame here along our spiritual journeys. There is only room for taking responsibility, which empowers you to change *any* situation or less-than-preferable encounter you find yourself enduring.

Another nice way to consider the power of taking responsibility is this. Your soul is calling out for experiences to evolve itself into the best possible "you" imaginable. You are creating people, places, and situations that call you to step up to the plate, make shifts, learn, grow, and find new places of strength you didn't know you possessed. Therefore, it is, in fact, you who is creating less-than-preferable situations but it's also up to you what you do with them.

I'm tellin' ya, Sally. It just feels so good to "own it".

Here's a great real-life example for you. Years ago I began to go into debt. I allowed someone I was dating to convince me to just "chill out" and not worry so much about attaining work. I worked less and less, spent more and more on my card (nothing crazy, mostly groceries and such), and eventually was at a point where I had to move into my car. (I'll be going more into the specifics of this transition, debt, etc. in the future but for the purposes of this example, this should be enough.)

Was it anyone's fault I had so little money?

No.

Was it anyone's fault I had to use my credit cards?

No.

Was it anyone's fault I lost my home and had to move into my car?

No.

It was, however, absolutely one hundred percent my responsibility that any of this happened. Instead of nose-diving into feelings of shame, guilt, self-hatred, and denial, I made the choice to say to myself, "Julie, you created this, which also means you can create yourself out of this. Something better is on its way because you have the power to make it so."

That doesn't mean my life was a bed of roses in five seconds. But what's most important is how my internal feelings shifted. We create from our energetic imprints, or feelings.

I began to acknowledge all the powerful and positive aspects of my life, shifting my energy from poverty and depression to joy and abundance. No one else could have done that for me. Just like no one else could have created my debt or other toxic situations in my life. Even if someone else racked up my credit cards, it would still be my responsibility. Somewhere in my soul's need to evolve, it would have created a situation where I learned boundaries, trust, and many other lessons from someone who uses my personal credit cards.

I'm responsible for my financial situation. I'm responsible, through my decrease of healthy food and movement, for the surfacing of pain in my left knee. I'm also responsible for everything else. I choose to accept responsibility for everything in my life, as anything else would deprive me of the power to shift any and all things as I want.

Taking responsibility brings an infinite horizon of possibility.

The best way to know that you're taking responsibility in your life is to ask yourself, "How do I feel when I take responsibility? Is it depressing (that's blame), or is it empowering?"

Taking responsibility is step one. Once you authentically do this, every other resource you need will be placed in your path to change your circumstances. The shift in vibration alone will make this happen. As each next step presents itself, you will be on your way to a new situation. By ignoring/denying/blaming yourself, you block all solutions from coming in to shift your life for the better.

Is there something you've feared taking responsibility for that you can "own" in this moment? The vulnerability and honesty of sharing this with someone you know is hugely empowering and just may help someone else with their own five second miracle!

Current Book – *Knowledge of Angels* by Jill Paton Walsh
Quote of the Day – "After all, the position of a reader in a book is very like that occupied by angels in the world, when angels still had any credibility. Yours is, like theirs, a hovering, gravely attentive presence,

observing everything, from whom nothing is concealed, for angels are very bright mirrors. Hearts and minds are as open as the landscape to their view, as to yours; like them you are in the fabled world invisible."
– Jill Paton Walsh from the book above

CAMPING ALONE (WITH ELK)

Day 296 – June 5, 2015

Three days ago I arrived at a campground along Lake Pillsbury, California. I needed to get away from work, as I had been working with no break since November of last year. I thought the campground would be packed for summer but perhaps the fifty percent reduction in lake water kept the people at bay. The camp manager said people may arrive today since it's the beginning of the weekend.

Upon arrival as the sun was setting. Not a single soul in the whole campground. Just the way I like it!

I arrived Tuesday night after work. The drive was twenty-six miles into the hills, mostly on a dirt road. I questioned my sanity once or twice and then kept driving. This place was chosen as a random point on a map that seemed to have water and was also very far from civilization (usually a requirement of mine when I camp). Upon arriving at dusk, I put my tent up with the wind whipping all around. The sun dipped its face behind the hills, a symphony of frogs began their harmonies, and crickets chirped into the dark night. As I placed my exhausted head onto my pillow I thought, "I am covered in coconut lotion. Perhaps I should sleep in the car instead of this tent lest a waking bear decides to have my tropical flesh for dinner."

I don't want to be scared of bears. I don't think I need to fear them for any sane reason. I have, after all, been hiking alone since I was thirteen without a thought about being chased by bears. Somehow, when I am camping in the boonies with no cell reception, a car full of peanut butter and honey, and skin soaked in coconut, it feels better to use my tent as a day spa and sleep in the safety of my car. I know some sort of nature vision quest or opportunity to overcome any hesitancy to tent camping alone (in bear country) is in my near future. For now, I'm taking my coconut-smelling booty into the car.

As I sit here, the tule elk are crossing the dry part of the lake bed to join the single elk I watched play in the water for almost an hour. It curiously left the safety of the forest to make a solo trip across open terrain to take a dip in what's left of the lake. My camp sits on a small cliff above the lake, so it's as if I'm watching a wildlife movie.

The tule elk coming in to swim and graze. My camp site is on the edge of this observation cliff.

All thoughts and words drifted into the ether as beauty realized itself in that perfect moment. The babies played and danced inside the barrier of elders. They screamed like little two year olds. I had never before seen evening "play time" or heard "call and answer" sessions between deer. Had I not seen the elk, I may have assumed children or birds were playing in the distance.

Not a bad view as the sun set over the hills!

The papas huffed and the mamas led the young to the water. At one point, an elk spotted me on the cliff. He stood and stared. Then more elk stopped and stared at me. Suddenly one of them let out a bark not unlike a large dog. It was the loudest "woof" I had ever heard. I sent them images that I'm gentle after a few more barks and eventually headed to bed as the darkness came. I fell asleep to the sounds of elk relishing the clean night air and water.

How often do we fall asleep with this sort of peace and state of relaxation in our hearts? I'm as guilty as the next one of falling asleep minutes after my computer goes off or after a few cyclical thoughts about work stresses. The moment I allow myself time in nature away from anything chargeable, I find my days and nights soaked in a relaxed state of tranquil wonder. It's not a lazy feeling. It's tranquility in the heart and a passion for everything I'm soaking in.

I vow to myself, just before sleep overtakes me, that I will experience this as often as possible. Elk, night air, the smell of lake water, and the sound of my heart guiding me home to myself.

Current book – *An Avalanche of Ocean: The Life and Times of a Nova Scotia Immigrant* by Lesley Choyce
Quote of the Day – "People who only buy their fruits and vegetables at the supermarket know nothing of real tomatoes. They eat stubbornly regimented, pinkish-orange tennis balls that merely resemble the tomato. I've argued nomenclature with greengrocers and they swear that these little obscene chemically-infested and colour-induced replicas are indeed of the same species. But I refuse to believe them. A tomato, I say, comes in an infinite variety of shapes and sizes. When

ripe it shines in the sun redder than human blood and carries with it a regal presence. When cut, it reveals the secrets of the universe, and when tasted it stings and refreshes and makes love to the tastebuds. So, how dare you insult my intelligence with these mere manufactured victims of chemistry, I pontificate to the man in Sobeys." – Lesley Choyce from the book listed above.

NATURE REALIZATIONS AND REALIZING MY NATURE

Day 296 – June 5, 2015

This morning I took a nice walk over to Oak Flat Campground, which was not nearly as nice as Sunset Point. As I walked, the gentle footsteps and calls of small tule elk brought a smile to my face. The area has been desolate since I arrived early this week, but I did happen upon three "city folk" dressed in yoga gear running along the road. Perhaps they're staying at a nearby resort I saw on a map. The image seemed odd, given no camp sites are set up with residents except me.

Incredible clouds sitting over the lake.

On the return walk to my camp, two dimes appeared in my path. I picked them up, turned around, and a nickel appeared. I somehow completely missed it even though it was right under my nose. I said, "Thank you," out loud and felt this was a sign that I am on path out here in the wilderness. Then just as I crossed the street to turn into camp a penny appeared in front of my toe. Keep in mind I am miles and miles from civilization on a dirt road. I sent another "thank you" out to the world and headed back to camp.

There are no showers here. Which means – you guessed it – I am indeed getting a bit ripe. Baby wipes, as I've mentioned in the past, are not a replacement for a bonafide shower. But I also don't care very much. No one is cuddling into my armpit at night; and I feel like a true camper instead of a "glamper". There is one hilarious ritual that takes place at night. Let's call it "spa time" during which I partake in a glorious facial regimen. I love the feel of creams, oils, masks, and other sundries coating my skin after a sun-drenched day. This, in itself, makes me feel as if I've cleaned up (and also as if my skin won't flake off). Self-care is extremely important.

Sometimes people have no idea how toxic they smell. I can often smell someone's head from the next aisle at work. It takes all my strength not to throw up as they corner me with questions. Like many other things, it provides an opportunity for compassion. People who do not take care of themselves obviously have a disconnect somewhere in their self-love circuitry. I'm no snob. I know sometimes we camp or miss a shower now and then. I know sweat is normal, healthy, and not to be feared. But there is a difference between the body's natural processes and people who do not take care of themselves. My time at work has been an interesting insight into just how many people stink.

Their diets pour out of their pores. Their teeth are rotten. I can often smell alcohol and pharmaceuticals seeping from their skin. My nose is extremely sensitive, which I am grateful for, as it allows me the pleasure of deeply experiencing taste and much more. But sometimes it can be a curse when I have to deal with filth about six inches from my face. These thoughts come and go as I write and notice my own need for a shower. At least I'm conscious of it, right? Ha!

Trail next to my campsite.

Today's thoughts seem so random. One theme, however, comes to me over and over because I am alone out here in the wilderness – doing nothing but reading and observing. The notion of being totally resonant with nature fills me every few moments, regardless of what is happening. I can imagine being a native person in this area, living near Pillsbury Lake, fishing, gathering, and truly connecting with my animal families. I already feel as if the heron who fishes from the same tree stump each morning is my friend. There are two bald eagles nesting about one hundred yards or so from camp. I watched one dive, catch an animal, fly it to a tree near camp, and then heard several babies screeching as they ate and thanked their parents. Seriously! Who watches this regularly and really "gets" that these creatures are all around us, connected to us, and we can live in harmony with them?

The first two camping nights the tule elk did not come. I eventually softened into the environment and the elk showed up, suddenly, with a sense of trust. Now the elk are sleeping in the sun below my cliff, taking an afternoon nap.

The bird life is so abundant up here. It's never entirely quiet. Something is chirping at all times. Most of the birds have kept their distance. This morning I tossed a few smashed blueberries over the cliff as a treat for my animal friends. As I read, sitting just before the cliff edge this morning, two chirping finch-like birds hopped onto the cliff. The lighter one (I assume female) was incessantly doing a vibratory chirp song, obviously a signal to the male. I believe it was a command to get her some food. The male hopped around and found a tiny worm, brought it to his mate, and she ate most of it from his mouth while he received only a nibble. This went on for fifteen minutes or more right in front of me. The male was so proud! He flitted and danced, bringing his Goddess several goodies.

Yesterday a giant fuzzy bumble bee crawled under my shirt near my waistband. I grabbed around when I felt the tickle, pulled my hand away, opened it, and the bee flew off without stinging me. I was incredibly gentle with no sense of panic. Typically, I squirm and slap away at something that's taken up residence in my shirt. Being amidst all of these beautiful creatures these last few days has increased my sense of peace and ability to stay calm and gentle.

Taking in a jaw-dropping sunset and realizing my nature.

I could write a list a mile long of all the wildlife encounters I've had since my arrival at good 'ole camp space eleven. For now, I'll leave you with these few gems in hopes you might take a bit more time out to connect with nature. For surely when we do, we realize our own nature. My pure internal nature feels grateful, serene, gentle, loving, and harmonious. How does yours feel?

Current Book – *Beautiful Ruins* by Jess Walter
Quote of the Day – "Even if they don't find what they're looking for, isn't it enough to walk together in the sunlight?" – Jess Walter from the book listed above

TRAINING THE ALPHA DOG THOUGHTS

Day 296 – June 5, 2015

"Writing machine" would be an understatement of a description for me lately. This is the third journal entry written in one day, though I've split them up here for easier digestion. Being in the wilderness pulls so many clear thoughts and feelings from me. I could likely write non-stop from sunrise to sunset, though my hand might not make it through (and you probably don't want to read a twelve hour blog).

Anypoo...

I'm quite lucky to be here during the opposite season from off-road vehicle use. During the colder months people can use various vehicles as well as motorcycles and this is usually accompanied by beer, cigarettes, guns, hunting, and drug use. There exists a culture that enjoys coming to the boonies and destroying nature. I'm not making assumptions. The evidence is all around. Notice the specimen below. I call it "beericus indicus" and its species graces the bottom of Pillsbury Lake, as well as the trails throughout the area. Tire marks rip through gorgeous tree-lined areas. Clearly people did not stay on the tracks but instead decided to tear through untouched land. Beer tabs and bullet holes line areas both on and off trail. I can't begin to imagine what the noise pollution does to the wildlife, so accustomed to tranquility.

I'm no prude. I certainly want people to have fun, drive fast, and get as wild as they feel they should. But I wish this would take place on a city track created for this purpose. Is it okay to abuse wildlife on behalf of fun? Not in my book. I know for sure I wouldn't ever camp here "off season" when unconscious people take over this land. One day I imagine this won't take place. I have enough trust in the consciousness of humanity to overturn the smut that's considered "cool" and "normal" on this planet.

Specimen found: beericus indicus, one of many in Pillsbury Lake.

I understand the need for cars, travel, etc. But I'm speaking to something else here. It's really about a culture that's perpetuated and various things within that culture that suppress conscious decisions. (In other words, it's not about the vehicles but rather the riders of them.) There is, indeed, a culture of people who teach their children that camping and nature are about tossing beer cans over the boat, putting bullet holes in trees, and driving as loud and fast as possible through uncharted territory. I suppose the question is – What do we do about it?

Instead of attacking people and telling them everything they're doing wrong, I simply try to be the example of what I want reflected outward. I create tranquility while in nature and observe the beauty all around me. I teach any children I'm with all about the sacredness of nature. There are those times we might witness something truly awful and need to call the police or confront someone, but I believe the very best thing we can do to perpetuate a higher planetary consciousness is to be examples of it.

Wildlife is all around. Let's live harmoniously with all the creatures surrounding us!

One of my favorite things to do is watch the shadows of lizards crawl up my tent while I'm resting inside. They even chase my finger and enjoy belly scratches from the other side of the tent material. Who knew? Now that would be a very wonderful thing to show our children.

While most of my thoughts and feelings have been incredibly peaceful out here, last night I allowed some tenseness to move through me without resisting it. There's nothing out here in nature to stuff down feelings or drown out painful thoughts. So now and then they arise. Not a big deal. It's really an opportunity to discover how to respond, and allow them to float up and out of the consciousness.

I felt the resistance to my job surface and the desire to quit immediately. This would not be wise right now, but I took note of the resistance and understand it comes from the knowingness that I'm working in a culture of people I don't resonate with. I also know I'm an entrepreneur at heart and anything less doesn't feel entirely congruent.

Specimen 2: miller lighticus drinkus

My mind and heart also drifted to my ex-girlfriend, as I've mentioned previously. I still have a physical sensation (not ever felt with anyone else) that happens when I think of her. It's like a physical swelling sensation in the heart, which often forces me to take a deep breath (Fast forward a year later. This no longer happens and it was indeed a sort of alignment between us versus resistance.). I can't explain it any other way than a heart-swelling manifestation of the love that exists between us. The fact that such a strong physical experience takes place is entirely new to me, so again I allow for it, observe, and release it. This is usually paired with tears and sometimes thoughts of past pain, but as time goes on, it is more purely a physical sensation and nameless emotion. I absolutely know getting back together would be toxic and not at all an option. So the continued depth of feeling is an interesting experience coupled with the knowingness not to enter into relationship beyond friendship. I find it very smooth, while in nature, to allow all of these thoughts and feelings to bubble up and release without my attachment to them. People fear admitting strange feelings or seemingly ridiculous things that surface. But we can't heal what is hidden.

Most of the time, while hanging out in nature, I feel blissed out. It's important to be transparent about thoughts and feelings that come up. Not every single thought is a bed of roses, though the key is allowing things to pass versus vortexing into them. One of the most difficult challenges people have is how not to be a slave to their thoughts. The thoughts become alpha dogs. Alpha dogs rarely change if beaten into submission or ignored, but they can be looked at and appreciated for who they are. We must, however, carry on with our own understanding that they do not control us unless we give them that power. I have a choice. I can train a dog to know I'm the pack leader or I can allow it to be my pack leader. I'm opting for the first option.

Voila. Be the pack leader of your thoughts. Notice when they bark. But certainly don't let them bark into infinity, so loudly you can no longer hear your heart speak.

Current Book – *An Avalanche of Ocean: The Life and Times of a Nova Scotia Immigrant* by Lesley Choyce

Quote of the Day – "Your lower self sees things from the viewpoint of your physical well-being only – your higher self considers your psychological or spiritual well-being. Your lower self sees you as the center of the universe – your higher self sees you as a cell in the body of humanity. When you are governed by your lower self you are selfish and materialistic, but insofar as you follow the promptings of your higher self you will see things realistically and find harmony within yourself and others." – Peace Pilgrim

DREAMING OF ARTICHOKES AT SUNSET

Day 297 – June 6, 2015

Something very special happens to me when I leave the crowds of the city and step into nature, or have delightful conversations in sleepy towns with people who are connected to the land they live on. I feel this same sense of connection and awakening as I read *The Telling Room: A Tale of Love, Betrayal, Revenge, and the World's Greatest Piece of Cheese* by Michael Paterniti. This book conveys a beautiful simplicity of connecting to the food we eat, the land its grown on, and the company we eat with. Whether we are vegetarians, vegans, or otherwise, the theme of connection (both to the food and the people) stood out to me while reading this book.

Mangoes and fresh air. Does it get any better?

While I've traveled extensively through Tasmania, France, Scotland, Wales, Ireland, and England, I deeply desire to visit Mediterranean regions such as Spain (where the book takes place), Italy, and of course my Greek and Turkish roots. I desire sitting with people, deep in conversation, who cultivate real food. I'd like to enjoy a beautiful raw feta with a wrinkled old Greek lady who teaches me her dances and her love of life. I'd like to talk to an olive farmer and watch him press virgin oil, only to drizzle it over tomatoes and basil moments later. I consider some people who only dream of sitting in a Vegas casino all day and night, eating buffet food with unidentified ingredients, speaking to no one but the slot machine. My heart wells up for them. They will never know the quiet joy of vacationing with locals, savoring not only the food, but the beam of light shared between each other's hearts.

When I come to places like Pillsbury Lake, there's a sense I'm getting closer and closer to the dreams I've shared above. I feel my senses come alive. My ears awaken after being dulled by traffic noise. My authentic dreams bubble up from places unknown. They've been pushed into veins, drowned in blood, clamored into cells with each unwanted moment spent slaving away in the workforce. But nothing will ever steal my dreams, no matter how deep they are buried. The pines will whisper them awake. The cool water will loosen and dislodge them from their hiding places. The wind will lift them out of the heaviness into the light of day. My desire to write, travel, connect, teach, think, feel, enliven, awaken, refresh, create and inspire – these are all welling up inside me.

View from a trail behind my lakeside camp.

My Crazy Creek Chair supports me as I dream into deeper places of myself and watch the birds fly by. Maybe there are a few readers out there who also desire this deep, connected experience of life and would like to travel to Europe. We could retreat together, adventure into pilgrimages, sit with divine hearts, and dine on divine foods. Maybe I am supposed to create a small retreat in which a group of loving, fun, spirit-based people join me in this adventure! Doesn't it feel wonderful to dream?

My little finch friends are back. I just noticed that crows often fly with their mouths open. Does the air flow create buoyancy? Is this a breathing technique? It is all so interesting to consider. I do not need to be "right". I don't need to Google it.

Isn't that how children theorize and learn? They pose questions, consider to themselves outcomes, and perhaps later research after making assumptions or predictions. We want to name it, define it, and explain it away before we've ever considered it. The wonders of life, for me, are like seedlings. They awaken ideas that ask us to question and dream into new possibilities. I can feel myself dreaming into what it must taste and feel like to enjoy a fresh grilled artichoke with Turkish people dancing into the sunset - the cobalt tiles reflecting their sumptuous hues, eventually matching the night sky. They blend together until night becomes still and so do the people.

Current Book – *The Telling Room: A Tale of Love, Betrayal, Revenge, and the World's Greatest Piece of Cheese* by Michael Paterniti
Quote of the Day – "At the same time, Ambrosio had given me a brief glimpse of a different, compelling sort of life, a life in which there seemed to be more time for family and conversation, for stories and food, a life I was desperate to lead now as an antidote to my own. It was okay to squander a day, a week, a year, sitting in that telling room,

summoning ghosts, because no one saw it as squandering. No, if you squinted a little bit, maybe what seemed like wasted time was, in fact, true happiness." – Michael Paterniti from the book above

THE ARRIVAL OF FELLOW CAMPERS

Day 297 – June 6, 2015

Three nights of an empty campground on Pillsbury Lake came to an end last night. The first folks to arrive had the decency to park two spots away instead of right next to me. (I have the best spot for sunset views, shade, and lake access.) The family who arrived last night consisted of a mother, father, and son. The son looked like he was about fifteen years old. It's possible he was older as his ears were stretched with rods and the first sound from his mouth was a belch from the beer he just slammed. He was a chip off the old block. His cigarette smoke danced behind him as he flipped his hair like a head-banger every few seconds to remove it from his face. His mom and dad were about fifty (going on seventy). Dad limped and Mom seemed to mimic his gait. She was covered in tattoos and her gray hair was long, dyed blonde with a layer of red crowing the top and roots. The three of them got wasted before heading down to the water with their canoes. I heard distant laughter and saw chains of smoke and canoes flipped upside down.

Cloud view from camp.

I love people. They're wonderfully fascinating. I wanted to sit the mom down and ask her, "Who is the bundle of goodness and big dreams beneath the smoke, beer, dye, and tattoos?"

I wondered who hurt her. Her energy reeked of pain and trauma. The boy was the embodiment of self-loathing anger. And yet there they were, falling off their canoes into the sunset and laughing their drunken tails off.

Later a lovely quiet young couple moved in next door. The whole campground was nearly empty and quiet. Any space could have been chosen. But they pulled up next to me because, once again, I had the best spot in camp. So the spot next to it was obviously second best. At least this couple was respectful and a little more in tune with nature (meaning they would never toss their beer bottles and cigarettes into the lake like the other family). The guy was as white as white could be. His partner was as dark as a night sky. They were both beautiful. Her voice was deep and husky. She was muscled from the canoeing and hiking she must do. I let them have their space but certainly enjoyed a stolen glance or two of her. I dreamed into romance and the confidence that someone great will join me at sunset, hands held, smiling and loving one another unconditionally.

View from the road near camp. That's what I call a good parking spot!

Behind my camp another couple arrived. I believe they were from Los Angeles. They were adorable and flirty. I wondered if this was their first camping trip. Their dog, Kona, was quiet and I wished I could cuddle her little lab-mutt face. The couple sat in the dry end of the lakebed, holding one another as the sun folded its eyes over the trees.

This morning I walked past two motorcyclists who arrived the night before. They obviously slept in after way too many refreshments. A warm pack of beer sat on the bench with two giant unopened Modelo cans. Upon my return hike into camp they were awake and enjoying a morning joint before cycling off into the hills.

I feel like I stick out like a sore thumb - Woman camping and hiking alone. Quiet and reflective. No charcoal. No meat. No nightly barbeques. No campfires. Lesbian with the side of her head shaved. Sometimes wears a head scarf. Layer of dirt covering her body. It's kind of hilarious, such a juxtaposition of me and most of the other campers.

This is nothing more than an opportunity to notice the energies around me. My descriptions help amplify the feelings I feel as I move through my surroundings. I know, intuitively and nearly immediately, who I want to associate with and who I do not. I observe, feel, consider, think, and assess. These are my practices as I wander through new areas. These are my practices while my car is my home.

Beginning of the hiking trail into the hills.

285

Many people ask me how I have little to no drama in my life and how I "know" the energy of people so quickly. That's tough to answer. I do know that I listen. And I trust what I'm hearing. It's not about whether people have tattoos or what drinks they drink. But often these things parallel how people move through the world. I surround myself with people who move through life with love, consciousness, peaceful intentions, and respect for nature. By getting quiet, observing, and listening to what my gut tells me, I get very clear impressions regarding who I should steer clear of. Because I listen, I eliminate nearly all drama and toxicity in my life. There is plenty of room for everyone in this world. I don't need to change people. But I do pay attention to the energies that surround me. If you don't want drama in your life, notice when you come across negative energies and steer clear. Noticing is alright. But wallowing in it, resisting it, or denying it will create drama. See it for what it is and then let it be. Move on until you feel a sense of alignment with the people you interact with.

I breathe deeply as I write this, soaking up the gorgeous hike I took into the hills behind camp. The various people surrounding me here make me chuckle. I smile, honor our differences, and send gratitude to the world for the goodness of every person in my life. I've chosen each one carefully. They're so full of love, support, and kind hearts. I cherish them.

I also send love out to everyone at the campground. May they step into the wholeness of their dreams and live a life of beauty and wonder. As a beer can pops open in the distance, the flames of night ignite, and the air becomes peppered with the sound of frogs; I retire to my tent to enjoy a meal of plain Wild Friends Chocolate Coconut Peanut Butter. It's all I have left except some protein powder and warm water. Ew. I will be eating well tomorrow upon my leave!

Pillsbury Lake will always be in my heart - everything from the tule elk pilgrimage to the funny people lining camp and coloring it with all the beautiful energies that make this world go round. My blogs are my letters to this world. I epistolize via the internet, hoping you might smile, cry, connect, love, embark, relate, and pass it forward so someone else may do the same.

Happiness in the trees!

Current Book – *The Telling Room: A Tale of Love, Betrayal, Revenge, and the World's Greatest Piece of Cheese* by Michael Paterniti
Quote of the Day – "Learn to listen to this silence, because it will tell you many things, unimaginable things, things of great beauty and meaning." – Michael Paterniti from the book listed above

COASTLINE BLISS

Day 308 – June 17, 2015

My time at Pillsbury Lake ignited the desire to experience as much time in nature as possible while I'm working up north. I'm working about thirty minutes south of San Francisco with easy access to water, redwoods, trails, elephant seals, and much more. I have no idea how long I will stay at my job. It's full of challenging people and situations but it's also providing me some freedom to see the world and begin paying off bills.

Back road between Pescadero and Half Moon Bay

The last two weeks have been spent wandering around the coast near Half Moon Bay and Pescadero quite a bit. When work ends I usually head to the coast, regardless of the time of day. Sleeping somewhere on the cliffs or in a sleepy town is much more peaceful than trying to find overnight parking spots in the busy town where I work. I also have the added benefit of watching seals play as the sun rises. It doesn't get better than that!

This is what my breakfast looks like at a nearby berry farm!

I'm so grateful for the wild coastline from Santa Cruz to Half Moon Bay. It's called "The Slow Coast" because its wide open spaces and meandering roads tend to make us take a breath, slow down, and get present. Each beautiful curve of Highway 1 beckons me further, yet also holds me in each lovely bend. There are several nostalgic spots I go to consistently. Swanton's Berry Farm in Davenport is the perfect spot for a picnic, fresh organic coffee, basket of berries, and a homemade chocolate truffle. Much of this book was written there. I also stop often at Harley Farm, as you've already read about, where I enjoy animals and take in the peace of the surroundings. There's also a fantastic thrift store in Pescadero and another in Half Moon Bay where I score a plethora of used books. These now familiar places have become my "home" of sorts. While I explore constantly, there are definitely places I reach to for that familiar sense of comfort. After a few months, one gets to know which places aren't worth going to and which ones can be relied upon.

The library in Half Moon Bay is another favorite spot to do work or read. Sometimes I wonder if the employees there know I'm homeless or if they just think I'm one of those rare birds with no internet access at home. Some of the people who are homeless are very obvious. Several frequent library users are fairly dirty and on some heavy duty medications. I see almost exactly the same crew every day I'm there.

There's a couple who live in their car and the man plays children's computer games all day. His wife (?) has been banned from hanging out there, I believe. I once caught her drunk or high on something at the laundromat trying to make out with a young Mexican man. Plus she was screaming and acting insane, so he had to make her go back to the car. I don't know if he was living with the couple as a helper or if they were just partying together. It was all very odd. All I know is "Ms. Thang" does not come to the library except to tell her partner a sentence or two and then leaves. I see the *strangest* things.

A teenager visits the library daily, plugs into the computer and proceeds to chew on this earphone chords for six hours or more while he plays war games. He smells like potato chip grease and unwashed hair. I had to leave once because I wanted to throw up in my mouth a little. I know that sounds harsh, but I could not take the smell. People always wonder what I'm exposed to during my life on the road. Hopefully this paints a clear picture of both great and also not-so-great things I experience.

At about 2:30 p.m. the children begin to file in after school. One huge race for computers begins and most of them do not leave their seats until 8:00 p.m. when the library closes. The stories go on and on.

On a good note, I recently found a book that was beaming a ray of light at me as I walked past the library entrance shelves (as I mentioned in a previous entry). As I turned and picked it up, I knew it was something I was supposed to read. It was called The *Story of My Heart* by Richard Jefferies. Immediately I knew this book about his love of nature would speak to a deep part of my soul. I've encountered so many similar experiences since surrendering to this journey. I'll do my best to share as many as possible over the coming months as well. Despite the loopy folks at the library, I'm so happy to have a place filled with amazing books, a place to do my work, and a place to people watch (crazy or otherwise).

I know virtually every Slow Coast coffee house, which ones have reliable internet and computer outlets, and which ones have drinkable coffee. One popular destination in downtown Half Moon Bay is an excellent place to do my computer work, but their coffee is awful and their restroom is so dirty I wonder how the health department allows them to stay in business (the cooks use the same restroom as the guests). It's usually my last choice for work; often my choices are based on clean restrooms. I liken a clean restroom to finding gold in an abandoned cave. Seriously!

Summer has arrived along with the hoards of people, but I'm an expert at finding desolate beaches. Sometimes it's a matter of waking early in the morning and other times I can find mid-day beaches with nearly no one. When I visit the elephant seals at the State Park, I make it a point to head to a beach below the cliffs. Very few people find it and there are flat open stretches of beach to run on.

My secret secluded spot!

Sunrise and sunset walks in Half Moon Bay harbor are also a favorite. While I don't enjoy seeing all sorts of beautiful sea creatures being stripped from the ocean daily, I do enjoy the salty air, friendly gulls, migrating whales, and the seals who seem to pop their heads up nearly every time I'm there. One of them comes close enough to pet as it begs for fish. These moments I wouldn't trade for anything. When I had a home and was going through difficult times, I'd usually bury myself in a movie or the computer after work. But my lifestyle has encouraged the experience of playing on the coast nearly every day. I feel as if I'm on a permanent road trip, and I love it!

Sunset over Half Moon Bay

Today I simply wanted to share the beauty I live amidst with all of the readers out there. For this I'm grateful and hope to charge up a few unused nature batteries out there. If you've wanted to hit the trail or the coast, don't wait! Ready...set...go!

Current Book – *Born to Run: A Hidden Tribe, Superathletes, and the Greatest Race the World has Never Seen* by Christopher McDougall
Quote of the Day – "You don't stop running because you get old, you get old because you stop running." – Christopher McDougall from the book above

CONSCIOUS LEADERSHIP

Day 315 – June 24, 2015

The company I work for prides itself on being a progressive, "conscious" business full of "conscious leadership" principles. Since arriving last November, I've seen very little of this. A couple of people I work with do indeed exhibit conscious leadership skills, but overall I'm shocked at how few. When I took this job I was excited to have leaders who align with concepts such as speaking and listening from the heart, using professional language, speaking with soft but direct tones, doing ethical things as examples to the staff, and making good choices even when no one is watching. I found the sign below at one of our leadership courses the company offered called "Conscious Leadership". Seems pretty straight forward, right? "Integrity – A conscious culture is marked by strict adherence to the truth telling and fair dealing. Integrity is doing the right thing even when no one is looking."

Recently all of the leaders of the teams gathered in what we called "the dungeon". A flight of stairs below our store led to a windowless room on cement floors, complete with fluorescent lights. We made do with the surroundings, though I can't say our meetings in this room did any wonders for the psyche of the attendees.

We were in a discussion about the current parking situation at work. Our store does not have enough parking for customers, let alone employees. The employees can park in a structure kitty-corner to the store, pay five dollars, and are reimbursed the same day if they choose. Thus, they can park for free. Their other option is to park several blocks away in the neighborhood, as our store has a contract with the city to leave the surrounding streets open for its residents. This bustling urban city needs all the parking it can get for the paying homeowners and renters, not the employees.

Unfortunately, most of the employees think it's perfectly fine to park across the street in the Safeway parking lot. There are signs posted throughout the lot that anyone not attending one of the businesses in that complex, or anyone parked over three hours will be towed. Fair enough. They are just as busy as we are. The leadership members attending our meeting that day were trying to figure out how to get the employees to stop parking in our own lot and also in the Safeway lot. Most of the people I worked with were morally at the bottom of the barrel. They couldn't care less if they were taking a customer's parking spot or using a lot that belonged to someone else. They had zero ability to tap into the heart of someone else and ask themselves how they would feel if someone was using their space without permission.

What were we going to do about this challenge?

Because I saw every single one of the leadership members parking in the Safeway lot, I very *gently* brought up the following.

"Do you guys think it might help the parking situation if the leadership parked in the paid lot or where they are supposed to as an example to our employees? They are following our lead, so perhaps this will help them see where they need to be parking. I think this aligns with our company morals of being a conscious leader, as well."

"Authenticity – Conscious cultures are marked by an absence of artifice and a genuine adherence to the truth. Authenticity is when the stories we tell ourselves are the same as the stories we tell others."

One would think I took out a knife and chopped a few heads off. The retaliation was insane. I, personally, parked in the paid lot and was reimbursed daily. Not a big deal. But people are so lazy, they can't walk one building further to park in the paid lot. They would rather park one building closer and risk towing, break the law, and be a poor model of leadership. Apparently my leadership did not care about our open door speaking policy and the fact that I am allowed to voice my opinions while being heard, respected, and calmly responded to.

One of the main leaders said, "Well, I'm parked on the side of the Safeway lot that's unregulated and no one cares if I'm there."

She was wrong. The entire lot was regulated, signed, and several months later all of the people parked in this lot were towed.

Follow leaders who are full of integrity, openness, and enthusiasm. I love this photo of my brother and sister, which captures the essence of healthy leadership. Photo copyright Cara Hoffenberg.

I mentioned that although our company doesn't align with the philosophy and practices of Safeway, they too, are a business and they too were started by someone with a dream. We may not choose to shop there or believe in what they're doing, but should respect their space and business just as we want to be respected.

One employee said, "F...k Safeway!"

I was so shocked, I wrote down what he said so I could later confront this with leadership. (Of course it was denied later and no one admitted to saying this.)

Then the member of leadership who said she parks in an unregulated part of the lot (as if that makes it morally better) said out loud, "Who cares about Safeway?! We're always at war with them anyway."

Conscious leadership, eh?

"War."

"Who cares."

"F...k them."

Wow. These were some seriously conscious people I was working with. All I wanted was for people to examine a new solution – to be the example of what they were asking from our employees. To begin doing what we were preaching.

Several people in the meeting continued to bully and berate me. I had never felt so unheard, unappreciated, and disrespected. This was a huge confirmation that despite what corporations often preach, their practices are often nothing like their claimed values.

The meeting attendees became very uncomfortable. The gal I mentioned above brought up personal agenda topics to try to tear me down. They were blatant personal attacks in an attempt to shift the focus from the fact that she was making unconscious choices.

The next week our meeting was about the subject of bullying, sarcasm, and communication in the workplace. I explained that I felt bullied in that last meeting and that no one cared about the fact that I was calmly seeking solution. Instead they began to cuss, deny, and slam me on a personal level. One of our leaders became very defensive and one gentleman in the meeting said, "I get what you're saying, Julie. It's not about parking. You're speaking to something deeper."

Nature: My battery after hard days!

I was very quiet and calm. People were looking at me with looks of knowingness. They could feel how I was being treated. After the meeting one guy said, "I could tell that was very difficult for you."

Other people showed some words of support and did not like the way I was treated. I shared this with leadership in a private meeting, explaining how I felt and that other people came to support me in private. I explained that I should be allowed to express solutions and opinions respectfully, as I did, and not fear sarcasm, retaliation, and personal attacks. One of our leadership members understood for the most part, but did not bring everyone together to talk things out and arrive at calm waters. He also continued to personally attack me on some level after I was sharing with him what I learned in our company class about conscious leadership and open door communication. I had not used any metaphysical, spiritual, or other religious commentary but he does know I'm a bit of a new ager and into energy. He said, "You need to be careful of what you say. Some of this spiritual stuff you talk about could be viewed the same way as the Christian lady who spouts off all the time."

Did he just really say that to me? I could have easily built a case around discrimination that very moment.

The only remotely "spiritual" words I used were "conscious leadership" and I heard those words directly from our meetings. I did not mention "energy" or "crystals" or "vibration" or "astrology". This was merely a way for him to threaten me on an emotional level and shut me up. I knew I would get nowhere with him, so I let it go. I also knew in my soul that my original intention was of pure consciousness, a pure desire to find a solution. All I did was pose a question. "What if our leadership did such and such?"

Sometimes ya have to puff up your chest and be who you are!

I left in tears that day after being attacked. I also knew my time there would be limited - which, of course, I knew before I started as I have no interest in working for other people. I'm designed for freedom. Writing, adventure, art, travel, speaking, sharing, loving, gathering, creating, and so much more! I stayed grateful for the money I was making and the few good souls I ran into. But I also began to feel the freedom-seeking aspect of myself being ignited. The flame was kindled. (This is a very important key. Often people sink into despair, victimization, and dis-empowering emotions permanently. We must allow ourselves to feel the feelings and then turn toward what we want.)

That was not the last time I was in very uncomfortable situations at work. How long would I have to stay at this job (or rather choose to)? Well, you'll have to hang in there to find out. This journey has just begun and I can't wait to share the rest of it with you!

Current Book – *The Story of My Heart* by Richard Jefferies
Quote of the Day – "I hope succeeding generations will be able to be idle. I hope that nine-tenths of their time will be leisure time; that they may enjoy their days, and the earth, and the beauty of this beautiful world; that they may rest by the sea and dream; that they may dance and sing, and eat and drink. I will work towards that end with all my heart. If employment they must have – and the restlessness of the mind will require it... They shall not work for bread but for their souls." – Richard Jefferies from the book listed above.

LISTENING TO MY INNER ORACLE

Day 332 – July 11, 2015

Today I feel deeply connected to this spiritual journey. Some days my attention is guided elsewhere but I always bring myself back to the essence of this journey. While I'm of course a physical being, it's the spirit within me that guides me like the Oracle at Delphi. No matter how far I stray, I always come home to my heart. Luckily, I don't stray often anymore. The twenty plus years of studying consciousness, metaphysics, and personal development have resulted in a massive tool bag from which I grab what I need. I feel especially grateful for that today.

Orbs in an old barn.

Yesterday was an incredible spirit-filled day in nature. I captured several orbs at an old barn inland from Half Moon Bay and later my gut prompted me to take a photo on the side of the road near some forested land. There was nothing particularly wild about it. I just knew I had to take a photo. So I pulled over and captured what looks like a dimensional shift, or presence, or…. I did feel something pull me to capture this and what a gift I received as a result of listening to that inner Oracle!

Dimension shift?!

The closer I am to nature, the more I "see". Nature is my temple. As my time there grows, the inner gifts I receive multiply. For example, yesterday I saw a whale at Pigeon Point Lighthouse. Then during sunset I was walking along some cliffs closer to Half Moon Bay and thought, "Wouldn't it be amazing if a whale passed by?"

As soon as that thought occurred, a whale surfaced for a glimpse and then disappeared. This morning I saw another whale at the lighthouse. It was like a whale festival on the coast for two days!

I've been noticing how perfectly things flow when I'm "in the zone" as well. In other words, these beautiful synchronicities happen when I spend time in nature, listening to my heart. Not only does the wildlife show up in divine timing, but I'll be called to serve in some special way or meet someone who resonates with me. Today I was running late to work (I'm almost never late anywhere. I chose the long beautiful route to work.) and walked past a guy sleeping on the cement in a narrow passageway. The city where I work does have its plethora of homeless people, but never are they curled up on a busy street a block from my work. This man looked dead. I clocked in at work and told them I was going to check on him for a minute (they didn't mind). He looked young and if he was my son, I'd want someone to call 911 if he was passed out. I can't imagine people stepping over his feet from 4:00 a.m. until around 10:30 a.m. when I got to work. Our first employees arrive around 4:00 a.m. for the morning shift.

I tapped the man's shoe and he woke up after a couple of short taps. My heart was pounding because I was so afraid he had passed away. I could not make out any breath in his chest. I said, "Hey buddy. You okay?"

He was a little shaky and his hand was cramped up underneath him as if he was partially physically impaired. He smelled dirty but not intoxicated. I asked him again if he was okay. He nodded yes. He kept saying, "Sorry. Sorry." He was rushing to get up and out of there, as he knew he should not be sleeping in a business doorway. I tried to slow him down a little and let him know all is well. I told him to find a safe place.

This gentleman looked Hispanic or perhaps East Indian, so I was unsure if he understood all my words. My heart felt for him. He felt like a sweet soul who lost his way and didn't mean to end up like this. I did not get the typical transient vibe from him. There's another guy who stands on a nearby corner with a sign that says, "need money." He leaves trash everywhere and cigarettes hang out of his mouth all day, falling to the ground. I can't believe people actually give him money. But the man on the ground did not have this toxic vibe to him. There was a sweetness about him, both in his apologetic nature and the softness of his voice. I should have given him some water or something.

Hopefully the young man made his way into the world with a little bit of faith that someone out there cares about him. Maybe it was enough to pick himself up and choose well for himself. Maybe not.

I can't control the results. I can only do what I can in the present moment and give people as much love as I have to give. Maybe someone will read this and check on someone who looks very sick (or possibly dead) and a life will be saved. One never knows. That's the beauty of attuning to the inner Oracle. You listen, you hear/feel, you follow the guidance, and life gets more and more beautiful by the minute.

Current Book – *Last Child in the Woods: Saving our Children from Nature Deficit Disorder* by Richard Luv
Quote of the Day – "In medieval times, if someone displayed the symptoms we now identify as boredom, that person was thought to be committing something called *acedia*, a 'dangerous form of spiritual alienation' — a devaluing of the world and its creator." – Richard Luv from the book listed above

HOW TO MAKE DECISIONS WITH EASE

Day 335 – July 14, 2015

My life is filled with interesting questions people ask. One of the most common questions I get is, "How do you *know* when to make a decision, or how do you *know* what to do when you're confused?"

Although there are too many things to list that I feel I came to share with people, one of the most important things is the path of surrender. The question above comes to me frequently, as I live a path of surrender and don't often seem to be agonizing over life's decisions. The universe answers my questions automatically if I allow for it.

Decisions can feel as graceful as a soaring gull.

I know. That sounds like a lot of spiritual mumbo-jumbo. But let me break it down. First, I live my life based on the following assumptions. If you don't have the same or similar assumptions, my process likely won't work for you, which is fine. Maybe your own process works like a charm. However, if you're reading this because you have pain, agony, or stress over decisions, if you find yourself often confused, if you don't know how to *know* something, or you feel lost – take a gander. Here we go. The foundation.

1. Everything is energy.
2. What I vibrate (think/feel) comes back as equal vibration (people, situations, experiences that bring me identical thoughts/feelings).
3. The universal energies (God/Spirit/Source/Love/Creator) are innately good and are *for* me, not against me.

Assuming the above, I practice the following steps to find my own personal answers, using my internal guidance system, coupled with signs that show up externally as a match to my energy. Answers are not something that have to be created. They are already in existence. Every problem or challenge has the answer within it. The universe holds every key to every lock. Your higher self knows everything your lower self has not yet accessed. *(On a side note...I heard a discourse regarding an experiment that was done. DNA was removed from people and taken to the other side of the world. When the owners of the DNA were shown images of pain or joy, the DNA on the other side of the world reacted **in advance** of the images displayed. The DNA shrank in "knowingness" of the horrible images to come and then expanded before the joyful images were shown. So what's the point? Well, you innately know everything before it happens. Thus, all the answers are right there in your consciousness should you choose to develop the tools to access them. I know this is a lot to take in. Don't stress over it. Just examine the capacity of your DNA/consciousness to know everything it needs to with **ease**.)*

Here is my five step process to help you make decisions:

1. Ask
2. Listen
3. Watch

4. Feel
5. Decide

Get quiet. Listen to what is already available within you.

Be sure not to attach to a time frame or expect to be in each stage for any specific amount of time. Sometimes you might ask and listen for months. If you don't hear an answer, keep watching for any signs that show up. Pay close attention to your internal feelings as thoughts come up or events take place that guide you one way or another. Ultimately, everything will be guided by a feeling of knowingness. The decision is nothing you have to "try" to make happen. The "efforting" disappears with decision making when you rely on how you feel. The challenge for most people is not being able to align with their feelings. They stay in the mind, attempting to "figure it out". This is where the listening and watching comes in. If you get quiet and really take in all of your sensory experiences, you will begin to discover your feelings about every situation.

Here is a real life situation of mine to help illustrate this process:

1. Ask – "God/Creator/Universe, I'd like to move toward my next step where I can live my dreams. Please guide me to the answer of whether I should leave this job and place I currently reside/work in." (This is the "not knowing" what to do. Do I leave a secure job that feels bad in a place that also is chaotic? Do I trust myself to leave despite some potential financial challenges?)

2. Listen – I do morning meditations or simply listen to whether I should leave. Often the answer arrives here with total clarity. If it does not, proceed to next step.

3. Watch – I observe the external things that arrive to meet the frequency of what I've asked. For example, two nights ago I saw a bunch of hoodlums pull up to the park I enjoy. One threw a bottle of water on the grass and the others looked like a bunch of trouble makers. This was minutes after I heard gun shots a block or two away. The next morning at the park this whole area was covered in trash. Yesterday, while parked at a stoplight, a guy dumped his energy drink out of the car, looked right at me and didn't care. Then his girlfriend threw a napkin out of the window. Minutes later at the gym a guy who had finished his workout came back to his car, took a giant beer can he must have had pre-workout, and threw it under the car. He looked right at me and drove off. My workplace during this time was also full of negative, angry, resistant personalities. (Gee, Julie! Do you think the universe might be giving you some guidance as to whether this is the "right" place?)

4. Feel – Feelings always give us our yes or no. All of this gives me a sense of tightness in my belly and chest. I feel resistance to my surroundings, not a desire to stay. I don't know (or have to know) where my next place is, but today my inner guidance system (gut feelings) tell me to move on. I don't have to "think" it out for weeks on end and write lists of pros and cons. I don't have to figure anything out through any traumatic or agonizing

process. I just need to get quiet, listen, watch what shows up, and tune into my authentic feelings.

5.   Decide – I made a decision in the moment to leave work and the town I work in. I did not put a date on it. I just came to a decision that felt very solid and expansive in my belly.

Thank you!

There's one extra bonus step that works magic. Thank the universe and your higher self for the answers. Be grateful and acknowledge the ease through which your decisions come. Continue to watch for any signs that induce feelings deep within you. And most importantly, follow the guidance when it appears. I could stick around my negative workplace for years, ignoring how I feel, and creating a mess of a life. The guidance brought me to the knowingness I must move on. I trust it and can now begin asking my next request. "Please guide me to the next perfect work experience in a place that feels aligned with my soul." And I begin again.

Will you join me in the silence as you embark upon your most important decisions?

Current Book – *Last Child in the Woods: Saving our Children from Nature Deficit Disorder* by Richard Louv

Quote of the day – "Passion is lifted from the earth itself by the muddy hands of the young; it travels along grass-stained sleeves to the heart. If we are going to save environmentalism and the environment, we must also save an endangered indicator species: the child in nature." – Richard Luv from the book above

BONANZAS OF BERRIES

Day 358 – August 6, 2015 – 7:30 p.m.

My recent travels to Oregon on the way back from a friend's Seattle wedding yielded some incredible berry-picking moments. The berries were so abundant I wondered how anyone in the area could go hungry during the harvest season. If anything, a person could do a blackberry cleanse, eating nothing but berries for a month, and harvesting the plentiful spring water available.

As I was lost in the delirium of this berry vortex, I heard full sets/blocks of information, as if imprinting on me so that I may share with you. It's slightly difficult to explain exactly how ideas come to me for these blogs, but more of them arrive on the whispers of the wind or dew drops upon a leaf than anywhere else. Ideas are not stirred over like stews simmering and waiting to be fully cooked. The blogs or journal entries are usually "cooked" before I ever begin. One could call them channelings of sorts. I typically get an inspired moment where an entire story, concept, and matching words are instantly available. I hear myself speaking small essays into my own mind, hoping I'll remember the inspired thoughts for later if I'm not near a pen and paper. I'm grateful to be a conduit in some way, that the universal energy that wishes to pour through me can trust itself into my field. I trust it. I trust the message. I trust the information that needs to be shared, even if it seems odd or edgy. A co-creation happens - because I don't question the inspiration that comes, I believe it trusts me to see it through. It's a divine union of some type. Here is what came during berry picking this summer.

Why is berry picking so addictive?

Why do families like to pick berries together?

Why does this "work" not feel like work?

So many questions. And many answers come, having a bit to do with the questions. But also I realize the questions contain the answers just by asking them.

As I slowly and consciously reached for the plumpest, ripest, juiciest, sweetest berry, leaving its brethren behind, I felt a surge of knowingness that greed takes all, impatience takes all, and haste brings a less-than-preferable result (sour berries).

I also enjoyed the strength it took to pull full thorns out of my skin. Why do I go through the pain in order to have the pleasure? Is this symbolic? Does all pleasure require navigating through pain? Are we taught they go together?

More answers come...
...not all plants have thorns.

...the slower and more presently I move, the less the thorns affect me. ...in retrospect the thorns are less painful than what I remember. So perhaps what I remember is not actually how it was. Maybe nothing was painful.

Bag 'o berries!

I sense the smell of the dirt, the dew on the leaves, the silence in the stillness. I breathe in so deeply, I can barely allow myself to let it go. Please. Let me breathe in some more, fill my lungs into eternity with this smell so any time of day I can breathe it out, experiencing it again as the cloud forms all around me. I'm drunk, entirely intoxicated by nature. I'm so in love with life, and the simple pleasures all around me.

I feel my Grandma Marge close to me (she passed when I was about twelve). "Ju Ju Bee...did you get a bonanza?"

"Bonanza" was her term for a high yield of berries. She had a vacation home in the Upper Peninsula of Michigan and I grew up picking "bonanzas" with her. I always found a bonanza. I loved berries so deeply that they loved me back to the same depth.

My lips are blue. I'm eating part of the batch as I go along. I get antsy and take a few berries that don't fall off the stem with ease. My mouth is sour and salivating. Be patient, Julie. Some berries fall as I pick them and this teaches me to share with the animals and devas. Perhaps I can ease their gathering chores by dropping a few more.

I wonder if bears sampled here last night.

Deer remind me about the power of respectful grazing. They sample most patches and move on to other shrubs without depleting the whole area they're working on. They innately know not to devour and deforest their home. What would happen if we harvested this way?

I'm suspended in each present moment as I pick each berry off the vines. The ripe ones make no sound as they release their grip. I suppose I make no sound as well when I'm ready to release my grip on something that no longer serves me. I simply release and allow. Isn't it funny to think back on all the fretting, weeping, and hysteria that accompanied the things/people we've released? This seems light years away from the place I am now. Release my home? Sure. No problem. Release relationships that don't serve my greater good? Sure. No problem. Release my attachment to having to live a specific way society designed for me? Sure. No problem. Silent releasing. Easy releasing. These things and more come to me as I pick and release each berry. Oh, how I love berry picking and all the extra "fruits" it feeds me!

Current Book – *The Story of My Heart* by Richard Jefferies
Quote of the Day – "I believe that one of life's greatest risks is never daring to risk." – Oprah Winfrey

ONE YEAR IN MY CAR

Day 365 – August 14, 2015

How incredible to think I've made a Hyundai Tucson my home for one full year as of today. What I thought would be a brief month or two catching up on obligations and seeking work resulted in a year of my best adventures yet! Writing is one of my many passions. This whole experience, ultimately, guided me back to my love of writing. Not only did I create this blog to help others stay close to their hearts while meeting life's challenges, but I've had about twenty or so book ideas since the moment I stepped into my car.

People ask me, "What do you do all day in your car?"

I have to laugh at that because I don't need to literally sit in my car all day (though sometimes I do when it's raining or to read and write). Sometimes I ask a person that question in return. "What do you do in your house all day? I mean, really and truly, break it down for me in hours."

The bulk of the answers are, "Go to work, come home, prepare dinner, put the kids to bed, get on the computer to check social media, watch television, go to bed."

Now and then there may be a variance such as gardening, exercising, or going to an event.

My life is really not that different from the average citizen. I just do most things from my car or have to do them in town. For example, I go to the laundromat instead of doing a load of laundry at home. If I had a home with no washer or dryer, no one would think this was odd. But because I have no "normal" house, people say, "Oh my God! How do you keep all your laundry clean day to day?"

I shower at a gym instead of a private home.

I prepare less food than homeowners, but have the option of a small gas cook stove. I eat a lot of fresh fruits and veggies, prepared foods from markets, and easy things to prepare.

As far as social media and television, I have a phone to connect to the world around me anytime and can always go to a library or coffee house for internet access. I'm grateful I don't have hours to drown myself in television. While everyone does that, I'm typically on a trail, at an event, reading, hanging out with someone I love, visiting State Parks, and anything else to nourish my soul. This blog is peppered with beautiful places I saw within just a few days.

All in all, I'm just a gal, working her booty off to reduce her bills like many other folks in this world. I happen to not have the added bill of rent, not necessarily because I "don't want" a house, but due to the massive cost of living near me. That coupled with my bills would result in absolutely no freedom, no fun, no road trips, no visiting family and friends, etc. I would be working to pay the bills, food, and rent. As I develop other avenues of income, that will all change. But I'm just speaking to the state of affairs upon moving into my car. I took one hundred percent responsibility for the situation I was in and can honestly say I feel like a million bucks!

Today I'm on a plane to Chicago to see several family members for a couple of weeks. All of my bills are paid; I have money saved, and have absolutely no financial pressure. I have so much money saved I chose not to use vacation time at work during these next couple of weeks. I may not be rich enough to buy a nice big house and property yet, but I'm well on my way.

My detachment from physical comforts forced the awakening of a deeper place within. If any of you are in this situation or may be at some point, trust that how you look at the adventure is how it will be realized. Do you look through glasses of love, excitement, spirit, and adventure? It may not be easy, but choosing an empowering perspective creates empowering experiences. I'm excited for this spiritual journey to reveal more insights like these as I delve deeper into nature, connection, and purpose!

Below is an entry about posting my first blog you read at the beginning of this book (which went live one year, to the day, after it was written).

My first *blog* launches at 2:34 p.m. It's 1:39 p.m. and I want to remember this moment forever. So many thoughts and feelings filter through me. This feels very different than launching my other sites, which were essentially business sites (not that this one isn't, it's just highly personal and connected to my journey on every level). August 14th is also sacred on too many levels to list. Some of them include:

- Two of my dear friends I met through a radio show share a birthday today.
- Another dear friend and her husband share an anniversary today.
- A college friend's birthday is today.
- A co-worker last night told me her birthday is today.
- While working on this blog post, several other articles and numbers I've run into mention this date.
- Apparently the first day of the Mayan Calendar started August 14th, 3014 B.C. while I moved into my car exactly 5000 years later. That's just cool. Come on now!

I do feel my nerves bubble up just a little. My ego thinks, "Oh no - people will think I'm a failure since I ended up in my car after launching two businesses over the last several years; those businesses must have sucked." Or, "This site won't make a dime. You'll be stuck working nine to five forever for someone you don't want to."

Then I set those thoughts aside lovingly and stay steadfast in my vision. The truth is, I've written blogs without a penny of return since last year. I'd do this work for free, and I did. And now I wish to use it as a gift and service to the world, perhaps helping others surrender versus fight their circumstances, and to help them align with their authenticity. I had to do this for myself in order to really be able to help others with these things. We don't often want to admit those horrible failure thoughts and pesky sabotaging ideas, but in doing so we strip them of their power so we can step into our own.

I feel fatigued because I went to a business dinner until 9:00 p.m. last night and had less than three hours of sleep. I showered at the gym around midnight, and was at the airport by 2:30 a.m. for a 5:00 a.m. flight. There are a thousand excuses not to launch the site today - inner fears, I'm on vacation for two weeks starting today, I'm "busy" with friends and family, I'm exhausted, blah blah blah. But this is a choice. I can do anything I choose and right now I decide that nothing will get in the way of my blog launching - nothing!

It was a chaotic morning. The computer at the airport and rental agency were not working properly, I had a goofy shuttle driver (one I

wouldn't want to be alone in a cab with), and I couldn't find the "remote parking" hotel front entrance where I was supposed to be picked up. (Seriously. I walked the entire building's circumference and found nothing but a restaurant sign, which was the lobby I guess, but it was locked.) I was in a vortex of craziness in the parking lot and finally the shuttle driver found me in the most logical spot (the shuttle stop). Why the hotel guy told me to come to the front door with my nine hundred pound bags is beyond me. Upon arrival in Chicago the rental gal sent me to the wrong car. More carrying bags extra distances unnecessarily. This was just the flow of the morning.

Often when I experience moments of madness while out and about, signs arrive to let me know all is well. For example, I often get confirmation through the number 34, my most lucky number. This was listed at the end of the car rental number today. Also the space was 176. I was born in 76 and often see these three numbers together for whatever reason. Note the message I received, "Your journey starts here."

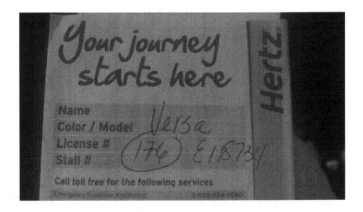

Goofy madness. Poorly run businesses. Crank-pots everywhere. But I kept myself sane, because I had some serious business to tend to! What business is that? This blog right here, of course!

I'm now at a coffee shop ready to launch in less than an hour. I pray from the deepest part of me that this site makes it to people who I may be of the greatest service to. I know I was gifted with the ability to write and speak/communicate because I'm supposed to help a lot of people. Of course I can't change anyone, but I can help people think of things in new ways, and with this comes change and empowerment.

I'm so excited! Giddiness is setting in. And I also feel like falling asleep. (Interesting combo. Kinda like a caffeinated heroin addict perhaps?)

I'm off to finish some tidbits; just wanted to record the combo of excitement and trepidation all in one here that I'm experiencing. Stay tuned for my upcoming book and many more after that! (YOU'RE READING THAT BOOK NOW!) Thank you to all of my angels out there who shared this journey with me over the past year. You are in my heart forever and I'm grateful to you all.

Website or bust, yo! Let's do this!

One year after moving into my car. Take a gander at my photo on the Day 1 blog and notice the difference. Life can be happy and glorious regardless of the external circumstances!

Book of the Day – *The Road of Dreams* by Bruce B. Junek

Quote of the Day – "Steve and Myia come out to greet us. They can't believe we are leaving – that we are actually doing it. Neither can we! We stand in their garage wearing our dripping rain gear and laugh as we tell of our 'official' departure moments ago. We seem so unorganized. Do we really think we can ride to Asia? The idea suddenly seems absurd.

We use up all their plastic bags to double wrap the contents of our panniers. We also shift the weight to balance our bikes and reduce the shimmies. Steve tries to convince us to wait for a better day.

'Be realistic', he says.

'If we were realistic we wouldn't be going at all,...'" – Bruce K. Junek from the book above

(*NOT*) THE END

That's correct. This is definitely not the end of my journey. I have completed a year living in my car, but this is not where my story ends. In fact, it's just the beginning.

As I assess the last year, chew it, and digest it, I realize there were bowls full of nutrients my cells utilized with delight. The list below is just the tip of the iceberg, but here are some of the things that were particularly nourishing to my soul:

- Went from miserable to happy in a "split second".

- Reconnected with nature.

- Rekindled old friendships and ignited new ones.

- Released mentorship that felt unhealthy and became my own beacon of light.

- Launched my blog website to share with others and began a foundation for my future business(es).

- Saw either a sunset or sunrise nearly every day for the last year.

- Slept on ocean cliffs, waking to swimming seals and howling coyotes.

- Wrote enough to fill two to three books.

- Realigned with my purpose more concretely.

- Healed from a past relationship.

- Traveled virtually every day to somewhere beautiful. I saw redwood trees, ocean parks, and did a road trip from Chicago to Michigan, as well as extensive coastal travel through Oregon and Washington.

- Hugged Amma (the hugging saint).

- Attained a well-paying job and took on the responsibility of four full time employees due to staff shortages, a job very few people could handle.

- Began hacking away at credit card bills.

- Eliminated my use of credit cards, paying nearly everything with cash or debit.

- Increased my self-love.

- Experienced more miracles than I can count!

This list is nothing to make small of. I'm really proud of everything that happened this past year while living in a Hyundai Tucson. Before I left my house, I had little to no feelings of self-appreciation, self-worth, and accomplishment. It wasn't that I hadn't done anything worth appreciating - rather I was feeling so low about the negative things I created in my life, they overshadowed my innate talents and goodness.

I snuggled into my layers of blankets each night, grateful for the incredible experiences I had. I thought about the world, tucked into their sofas or beds, drowning out their days in television or internet frivolities. There is obviously a time for both and I enjoy these, however I know most people use them as a form of escapism. They don't want to look at the realities of their lives, or hear the realities of their thoughts. They don't know how to listen to the deep voice within, telling them to wake up and live the life that's buried in their cells. And I can speak from experience. I lived through many nights watching television to avoid the reality of my bank account, the jobs I hated, the relationships that were unhealthy, and the fact that deep down inside I felt as if I failed myself.

My Hyundai Tucson symbolizes freedom from all of the pain and denial. There is no television in my car. I have to be silent most nights to avoid being spotted by members of the community (unless I'm parked somewhere desolate like the coast). Thoughts and feelings surface often. I see and hear them and allow them to move through me. I allow for healing to take place. Sure, I jump on Facebook to connect with loved ones and to share the beauty I experience along my journey, but I'm living my life without escaping the truth of who I am. I'm Julie Cara Hoffenberg. I'm a great and magical soul. I'm loving, loved, worthy, divine, and full of gifts to share. I'm a being - of service to the world. I'm a communicator. I'm also beyond words and definition, an energetic presence shape-shifting through life. I speak and write. People listen - because I'm clear, and they feel my authentic belief in my words and the love I have for them in my heart. I'm all of this and none of this.

One year in my car allowed me to realize myself back into the gifts I came to share with the world and the bliss that naturally bubbles up from my soul. I'm truly grateful to Mother Earth, for she is, I believe, what gave me the space to heal. She's like a big soaking spring, allowing me to bathe in her healing waters, releasing all that no longer serves me. Her minerals replenish me and the sounds of her soft streaming voice remind me she's always here for me, that I'm never alone.

As of August 14, 2015 (exactly one year after I left my home), I'm still without a home. People ask, "What are you going to do? Are you going to move to a more affordable area? How much longer will you have to live this way? Aren't you scared someone will break into your car? Will you stay at your job? If not, what will you do with your life? How will you make money?"

The list continues. People worry for me because I don't worry for myself. I choose not to participate and therefore nothing "bad" comes my way. "Worry" has been likened to "negative goal setting". I can't remember where I heard that phrase but it stuck like glue. The fears people have deep down in their souls cause repetitive thoughts and unnecessary worry. What's interesting is people fear I'll be hurt because I only have the four walls of my car to protect me. I have no alarm system or any other fancy personal protection gadgets. Meanwhile, many friends and family members are under the protection of the four or more walls of their homes and they don't feel any safer than me. They have extensive alarm systems and even with those alarm systems, they still have feelings of fear. They constantly check their alarms to be sure they're set. They worried before they had an alarm system and then after getting the alarm system, they still worry. So they added video monitoring. They fear break-ins. They fear theft. They fear their loved ones being harmed in the night. And that's all fine. I'm not saying they don't have a right to their fears and concerns. But certainly having a home does not ensure anything safer than a car. If anything, the bigger the space to protect, often the more people fear theft and loss.

There's an addiction to fear and worry. Chemicals are released in the body. They rush around, charging people with an energy that, while not always pleasant, is nonetheless addictive. The dramas that come with fear and the attention people receive for their concerns is also addictive. If people were not addicted to being fearful, would they *ever* watch the news as often as they currently do?

Of course not!

They watch the news. They discuss the horrors of society. They have fear regarding those horrors. They discuss the new horrors. And the cycle repeats. Several hours later they turn on the news again.

But I digress...

That was merely to illustrate the addiction to fear and worry. It's one of the most powerful drugs in the world. A great question to ask yourself is, "What would my life look like without this fear?"

So when someone fears a murderer will bust my car open and chop me into pieces for no reason, I wonder, who would this person be without these horrible thoughts? How much more joy, bliss, trust, and positivity would they have in their lives without wondering when someone is going to do me wrong?

Here's the actual *fact*. No one has tried to harm me in the year I've been in my car. This is what I focus on - "I am safe, cared for, protected, and loved at all times."

I also keep bubbles of light all around my car and use extreme caution and intuition when parking and frequenting new areas.

So I ask of you - instead of worrying for me, just love me. Know that I'm safe, cared for, protected, and loved.

Another big question I've received over the last year is, "*How* did you become homeless in the first place?"

This seems to be a bit illogical or unbelievable to people because of my background. I've been a business owner, empowerment coach, natural health expert, teacher, life insurance agent, and much more. Essentially what people are thinking is, "What's your problem? You have all this education and wisdom. How could this have happened? What did you do *wrong*?"

There's a whole lot I did wrong (if you want to call it that), but I don't view it that way. It was all divinely perfect to allow me this experience so that I may share on a deeper level with those going through similar circumstances (or those who wish to avoid them). I had worked with a lot of clients who were in desperate situations, sharing information on how to trust the universe and view every negative experience in the most adventurous and positive light possible. But I hadn't yet experienced the depth of what they had. I had talked about natural healing in the face of deep depression, knowing drugs are often unnecessary. Yet I hadn't truly done this for myself. I had only witnessed this in others' lives. Like I mentioned in the intro of this book, I brought back some serious medicine. That's a good enough reason for ending up in the situation I created for myself.

I considered putting the timeline of "how" I became homeless in this book, but it didn't feel right. The essence of this book is about the spiritual evolution from pain to healing - and how fast that can take place when people go back to nature, connecting with their truth and the people they love, and igniting their sense of passion/purpose.

You'll have to wait for book two of my spiritual journey to learn exactly "how" I ended up homeless. For now, take the gems I've dug up from my soul and apply them to areas in which they might help. Consider going to nature alone. Regularly. Get quiet if you go. Consider connecting with loved ones you've neglected recently. Consider asking your higher self what you came to share with the world, and then share it in any way you can. I promise your life will never be the same (in a good way, of course)!

I'm thrilled to share year two of my spiritual journey with you. Do I get a home? Do I keep my job? Do I stay happy? You'll find out as you join me on my journey. Know that I'm always with you. When no one understands your intuitive decisions that don't make earthly third dimensional "sense", know that I will. When you feel alone and unloved, know that I'm loving you and cheering for you. Your gifts are needed. Your spirit is needed. May your spiritual journey be ever-expanding.

I love you.
Julie xo

REFERENCES

Angelou, Maya. "Love Liberates" video. www.YouTube.com.

Byrne, Rhonda. *Hero.*

Canan, Janine. *Messages from Amma in the Language of the Heart.*

Chopra, Deepak. *Buddha.*

Choyce, Lesley. *An Avalanche of Ocean: The Life and Times of a Nova Scotia Immigrant.*

Cornell, Judith. *Amma: Healing the Heart of the World.*

Dyer, Wayne. *I Can See Clearly Now.*

Flannery, Tim. *Among the Islands: Adventures in the Pacific.*

Edward Sharpe and the Magnetic Zeros. "In the Lion"

Francis, Myrtle Shepard. *Theodosia: The Flower Wizard of California.*

Hillenbrand, Laura. *Unbroken.*

Hubbard, L. Ron. *Clear Body Clear Mind.*

Hubbard, L. Ron. *The Way to Happiness.*

Jeffries, Richard. *The Story of My Heart.*

Junek, Bruce. *The Road of Dreams: A Two-year Hiking and Biking Adventure Around the World.*

Katie, Byron. *Loving what Is.*

Kerouac, Jack. *On the Road.*

Larson, Christian. *The Pathway of Roses.*

Luv, Richard. *Last Child in the Woods: Saving our Children from Nature Deficit Disorder.*

MacLaine, Shirley. *The Camino: A Journey of the Spirit.*

McMahon, Susanna. *The Portable Pilgrim: Seven Steps to Spiritual Enlightenment.*

O'Reilly, Sean and James. *Traveler's Tales: The Road Within – True Stories of Transformation.*

Schlesinger, Jillian (director). *Maidentrip*, 2013.

McDougall, Christopher. *Born to Run: A Hidden Tribe, Superathletes, and the Greates Race the World has Never Seen.*

Nichols, Wallace J. *Blue Mind.*
Paterniti, Michael. *The Telling Room: A Tale of Love, Betrayal, Revenge, and the World's Greatest Piece of Cheese.*
Price, John Randolph. *The Abundance Book.*
Ryan, Tom. *Following Atticus: Forty-eight high peaks, one little dog, and an extraordinary friendship.*
Stanek, Gerald. *The Road to Shambhala.*
Strayed, Cheryl. *Wild: From Lost to Found on the Pacific Crest Trail.*
Walsh, Jill Paton. *Knowledge of Angels.*
Walter, Jess. *Beautiful Ruins.*
Yogananda, Paramahansa. *Autobiography of a Yogi.*
Virtue, Doreen. *Unicorn Oracle Deck*.

ABOUT THE AUTHOR

Julie Cara Hoffenberg's art, writing, and all creative endeavors attempt to bring about new thoughts, feelings, and cognitions to her audience. She doesn't try to force anything, but rather listens, writes, feels, considers, and lets go. Perhaps someone will be there to receive a word, image, or thought that leads to an empowered shift.

On her journey of self-described course corrections, her passions are infinite. She resists boxes, constantly engaging with and playing with life. Nature is Julie's temple. It's where she draws most of her inspiration and deepest sense of connection to all that is.

You can find her on a trail, in a van touring the world with her wonderful wife, watching people's pets, philosophizing with friends about all things metaphysical, or laughing hysterically as she imitates life's funniest and strangest humans. Her astrological cocktail of Pisces sun, Scorpio moon, and Gemini ascending encourage her to love deeply, explore all life has to offer, and intuit more than most of her friends realize. She's sending you a great big hug from her heart right now, hoping you realize your magnificence!

Coming soon! More books and artwork by Julie Cara Hoffenberg!

Visit www.JulieCaraHoffenberg.com for all upcoming projects.

If this book helped you in any way, please purchase one (or fifty - wink wink) for someone you love! Julie would love to hear how this book served you and receives mail at:

P.O. Box 293 Ojai, California 93024

Made in the
USA
Columbia, SC